PRAISE FOR "WISDOM, WELLNESS AND REDEFINING WORK"

"In *Wisdom, Wellness & Redefining Work*, John and Greg teach leading-edge methods to train our brains to optimize our performance, and increase our vitality and quality of life in the process. All organizations of any size will benefit from enhanced engagement and innovation by implementing these proven principles. An important read for all in this stress-filled world."

Stephen M. R. Covey and Greg Link
authors of *Smart Trust: Creating Prosperity Energy and Joy in a Low Trust World*

"In this intriguing book, John Selby and Greg Voisen offer the interested reader an opportunity to explore the power of mindfulness and the mind-body connection in the demanding environment of the workplace. Based in the latest research from science and psychology, their methods are easy to follow, and hold real promise for transforming each individual's work experience and productivity, as well as raising the possibility of creating more compassionate and caring organizations. I encourage you to try their approach and see for yourself!"

Dr. Jeffrey Brantley
psychiatrist, professor at Duke University, and
author of *Calming Your Anxious Mind, Five Good Minutes*

"John and Greg have developed a powerful wellness-productivity program based on a set of 30 universal values called Focus Phrases. By holding one of these Focus Phrases in mind during a workday, employees and leaders alike can focus on their strengths, stay in tune with their inner voice of inspiration, and enjoy their work while performing at higher levels. The WizeWell Process will help companies shift from greed-fixation to service-dedication, step by step stimulating a brighter, healthier, and more innovative work environment."

Lance Secretan
author of *The Spark, The Flame, The Torch*

"*Wisdom, Wellness and Redefining Work*" is a compelling roadmap to creating vitality in the workplace - for yourself, your teams, your company and your greater ecosystem. John Selby and Greg Voisen invite readers to discover a hopeful path filled with energy and vitality; they outline can-do practices and processes for moving along this path. This insightful book illuminates the essential human and humane foundation of business. The WizeWell Process enables employees to aim their power of focused attention regularly toward awakening their full humanity in the workplace; this will help to create more resilient, sustainable, and successful businesses."

Jeff Klein
author of *Working for Good*, Host - It's Just Good Business, Trustee - Conscious Capitalism, Inc., Producer - Being Human 2012

"This book brings awareness, clarity and understanding to the challenges we face regarding the healthcare crisis. It introduces an important new program for any company executive seeking to effectively manage job stress, the leading cause of increased healthcare claims. The WizeWell Process is designed to gently but surely, over time, help employees focus more effectively, maintain higher energy and creativity, and enjoy their work - and it accomplishes this goal with minimum cost and training time."

Dr Daniel Amen
author of *The Amen Solution*

"In these times of increasing turbulence and uncertainty, and in a world wrought with a myriad of problems stemming from decisions lacking in wisdom, we are constantly reminded of the need for deeper wisdom to inform our decisions and guide our lives, work, and organizations. Voisen and Selby have done their homework; this book offers a wealth of well-grounded insights, skills, and research, inspiring their readers to apply its lessons to their lives."

Dr. Joel and Michelle Levey
Founders, WisdomAtWork.com, authors: *Wisdom at Work;*
Living in Balance; and *Luminous Mind*

Tapping Higher Vitality & Innovation

Wisdom, Wellness & Redefining Work

Thriving In A World Of Increasing Complexity

John Selby / with **Greg Voisen**

Wise o|o gie

Original Copyright 2011 by John Selby

Distributed by Wiseologie Media Group,
a subsidiary of Wisdom Nook Publishing LLC

Book (Print): ISBN 978-0-9846777-8-8
Mobi (Book): 978-0-9851907-0-5
Epub (Book): 978-0-9851907-2-9
Published and printed in the United States of America
Published by Wiseologie Media Group, Carlsbad, CA 92010

For contact information, visit www.wiseologie.com

Overview

~~~~~~~~~~~~~~~~~~

For America to re-ignite and expand its stature as the world's economic leader, its leading companies must apply new insights and methodologies from cognitive research to help employees side-step stress, boost wellness, and access higher levels of ingenuity, compassion, wisdom, and integrity.

By introducing specially-designed cognitive 'breather breaks' into the work environment, companies can proactively reduce the mental component of stress, and in the same process maximize employee focus, performance, and satisfaction.

This book will explore a new cognitive method to help everyone on your team access their higher creative potential enjoyably and on a regular basis – as they manage their all-powerful focus of attention and learn to stay in the zone more often at work. Insurance costs will go down as innovation and productivity rise up.

~~~~~~~~~~~~~~~~~

WizeWell Value Sheet

~~~~~~~~~~~~~~~~~~

The WizeWell Process explored in this discussion is delivered as a short daily multi-media insert into the corporate workplace, generating stress reduction and focal enhancement via an innovative set of Focus Phrases that periodically retarget employee attention in highly beneficial directions. The program costs pennies per day per employee; is non-intrusive and enjoyable; and accomplishes the following valued goals:

- **Improvement of employee focus and performance**

- **Reduction in stress-related medical costs**

- **Higher motivation and innovative thinking**

- **Fewer stress-related errors and accidents**

- **Heightened empathy and customer satisfaction**

- **Enhanced employee vitality and enthusiasm**

- **Reduced employee dissatisfaction and turnover**

- **Brighter team spirit and employee fulfillment**

Based on new medical and psychological research (as reviewed in this discussion) the WizeWell Process stimulates major advancement in employee focal power and mind management. Requiring only minutes a day for training and reinforcement, the process predictably boosts employee engagement, wellness, job satisfaction, mental clarity, wise action, empathic relating, stamina, and other performance/success elements.

~~~~~~~~~~~~~~~~~~

Table Of Contents
~~~~~~~~~~~~~~~~~

Foreword by Marshall Goldsmith

~~~~~~~~~~~~~~~~~~

With *Wisdom Wellness and Redefining Work*, John Selby and Greg Voisen describe the WizeWell Process they have developed for long-term application at work. This is a new incremental wellness-innovation method designed to help teams actively reduce psychological stress, access their higher creative potential, and manage their focus.

In the last few years, in my work with hundreds of companies around the world, I've noticed that many people are less engaged at work (and at home) than in the past. This book offers a method to combat this apathy, and reduce stress. The authors of this book show employees how to more successfully manage their focus of attention each new day, in order to respond to at-work situations with less stress and fatigue. Within this same process, employees are able to access greater vitality, creativity, innovation, and intelligence. This is a great trade-off!

We all seem to want the same basic things from life. But why do we then regularly do the opposite of what it takes to achieve our deeper goals, maintaining misery instead?

When I ask people, "What really matters in your life?" they usually reply with health, wealth, relationships, happiness, and meaning. It's interesting to note that, even though everyone claims to want happiness, meaning, creativity, and intelligence, our most common everyday process – what we do more often than anything else – is continue to do what we were already doing … repeating patterns that get us nowhere.

John and colleagues explain that the reason most of us get stuck in inertia is that our workplaces have become progressively more stressful – and at the same time, for many employees work has become less rewarding. They are required to work harder, do more, and do it quicker, faster, and for longer periods of time. The end result of this constant hurrying and driving is a reduction in performance, energy, and spirit.

The WizeWell Process is a great solution to stress and dissatisfaction at work. John and his team have identified 6 core themes and 30 essential Focus Phrases that address the stress crisis in a productive, meaningful way. This is great news for many employers, as its daily use can benefit the organization through generating employee performance-improvement, fewer errors, enhanced vitality and enthusiasm, and much more.

The program is also great news for employees who may, in the process of applying the program, discover the illusive experience that all good employers want for their employees – employee satisfaction.

Give this method a try – you and your organization have everything to gain!

Life is good.

Marshall Goldsmith

Marshall Goldsmith is the million-selling author of the *New York Times* bestsellers, *MOJO* and *What Got You Here Won't Get You There*. He was recently recognized as the *Thinkers 50* most-influential leadership thinker in the world.

Introduction

Stressed Out Or Innovative?

Click Here to Watch Intro Video

Seldom have times been so tough, and at the same time the opportunities so high. Incessant change, flat paychecks and a steady decline in wellness and satisfaction are seriously eroding our workforce assets. The result is chronic stress – and stress is the great killer of wellness and innovation. Realistically, how can your company act to reduce the root cause of stress, and initiate a steady surge of healthy creative energy throughout your workplace?

The intent of this discussion is to examine a new proactive approach to re-focusing employee attention beyond stress-generating mental habits and related emotions, toward more positive present-moment participation in the unfolding of your company vision.

- Our new approach to stress reduction and performance enhancement is based on recent breakthrough research in cognitive science; you can overview the key research papers in the last forty pages of this book. The at-work methodology that's emerged from this research carries the pragmatic power to quickly recharge the body and refocus the mind with renewed vitality, clarity and creativity.

During the last decade, as our understanding of work has been provoked into super-rapid evolution, business executives and psychologists have come to agree that the prevailing mood, focus, intent, and health of one's team is the pivot point of every organization's success. Stressed-out employees who feel unhappy and unhealthy at work will pollute a company's atmosphere with negativity – and drag that company down.

Conversely, a company of healthy team players who enjoy each other's presence, share common core values, respect and support each other – this is predictably a company destined for greatness.

- Specifically, the attitudes, emotions, expectations, and mental focus of each employee determine what actually gets accomplished each day.

Numerous studies (see scientific appendix) document how employee focal skills play a key role in all aspects of a company's success – and yet to date there has been no effective approach for maximizing this 'focal factor'. This discussion explores the theory of focal enhancement, and the availability of practical tools for helping employees manage their focus of attention consistently and correctly. By employing such tools on a regular basis, workers will feel less stressed-out, more healthy and productive – and more satisfied with their work.

Recent perceptual and cognitive studies have proven the surprising power of a particular set of mental-focusing techniques (traditionally called mindfulness meditation) to effect positive changes both mentally, emotionally and physically. This ancient mind-management technique, even in its original format, has been proven in medical studies to carry the power to positively impact a great number of current ailments in our society, including obesity, heart disease, diabetes, anxiety, depression and other mood disorders, drug-abuse, ADHD, chronic pain, gastrointestinal disorder, brain-tissue recovery, etc.

Of equal importance to the business world, related studies have demonstrated how fine-tuned mental-re-focusing techniques can relieve fatigue and stress, boost mental clarity and innovation, lower errors and accidents, and help employees function 'in the zone' more often at work.

- In our scientific appendix of 57 key research papers you can review research by HIH and other medical institutions verifying the proven power of this special mental-re-focusing process.

The question naturally arises: now that formal research is in hand proving the effectiveness of this mental-focusing procedure – why aren't these procedures being employed in the workplace?

The main implementation problem has been that the original source of these focusing techniques, traditional meditation, takes half an hour to move through and is often associated with religious organizations and beliefs – plus the process is quite difficult for most everyday Americans to master.

New Focus-Phrase Technology

For the last decade, John Selby and colleagues have been experimenting with new short-form at-work mind-management procedures that isolate the active psychological ingredient in traditional meditation – a temporary state of mind called 'mental silence' or thought-free attention. The program being introduced here is a stream-lined, inexpensive, highly-effective methodology that merges mindfulness meditation and cognitive science into a short-form high-performance process that all employees can readily learn and apply at work.

Specifically we're going to introduce what we call the Breather Break, where employees pause and quickly recover from stress and fatigue, and regain mental clarity, emotional balance, and focused motivation.

- In just 2-3 minutes during a guided Breather Break (via computer, print or mobile delivery systems) employees move through an enjoyable re-focusing process that shifts them rapidly out of over-stressed chronic-thought mode, into a present-moment whole-body focus often described as 'in the zone'.

A Breather Break, which is scheduled 1 to 4 times during an average workday, begins with a key 'relax and recover' step that takes just a minute or so to accomplish once your employees get good at the process. The second part of a Breather Break involves an enjoyable momentary focus on one of 30 special Focus Phrases. These Focus Phrases are the active ingredients in the Breather Break process.

This is where our program expands beyond mindfulness training into a uniquely-powerful cognitive technique for focusing and strengthening your company vision. We've identified a set of core principles, shared needs, fundamental attitudes, and basic psychological requirements that everyone ideally aspires toward, but in practice mostly forget to hold in mind and thus manifest.

Quite distinct from positive affirmations (which are hopeful imaginations about a future goal), Focus Phrases are realistic verbal pointers that aim a person's attention directly toward universally-accepted needs and intentions.

- Research shows that people who hold positive beliefs, attitudes, expectations and thoughts in their minds are more productive, healthy, empathic, successful, and satisfied with life than people who fixate overmuch on negative thoughts, attitudes, and expectations.

By inserting a new Focus Phrase into your work environment each day for 6 weeks (a full cycle of the program) you guarantee that your employees are regularly focusing their attention in the key psychological directions that sustain a healthy company.

Later in this book and in more depth in the accompanying Guidebook, you can review the 30 Focus Phrases we're introducing as the heart of our program. You'll find that each of these Focus Phrases, when said silently to yourself while you stay aware of your breathing, instantly aims your attention toward an actual experience of the targeted life theme.

Why Breather Breaks?

Numerous cognitive studies have shown the obvious – that at-work focus of attention is not a constant. As an average morning or afternoon at work progresses, an employee's focus of attention steadily loses power – and productivity, clarity, and creativity wane as a result. Attention wanders from the present-moment work at hand into thoughts about the past or the future; errors and accidents become more frequent – and work either doesn't get accomplished, or is not done well.

- Unstructured coffee-breaks have traditionally been offered to employees who are approaching low-performance awareness levels – but without any intent-driven structure, such breaks usually fail to encourage necessary shifts in mood, intent, and focus.

Breather Breaks guarantee that employees are regularly guided in directions that they themselves value – as they regain their physical vitality and enjoyment of the moment, recover from the fatigue of constant point-fixation work, and shift into integrative whole-body clarity.

Once this inner shift has been accomplished and psychological stress reduced, the Focus Phrase Of The Day serves as the interface between employees and the wisdom of both their employers, and what is called the perennial philosophy – that universally-agreed-upon wisdom about what's most important to focus on in life if we want to remain healthy, financially successful, and fulfilled deep-down in our work challenges.

From an employee's point of view, Breather Breaks are a much-valued gift from their employer. From their employer's perspective, Breather Breaks are indeed a recurrent gift to employees, offering much-needed emotional and mental relief. But at the same time, Breather Breaks represent a wise investment of time and money with the clear intent of training employees to perform at more creative levels of engagement.

Breather Breaks also express another core scientific finding about employee performance and mental habits: in order to change old behavioral patterns that are inefficient, it's always necessary to establish a reinforcement system that continues to remind and refresh a person about the new approach being learned. Reinforcement is key!

- For instance, each time a person moves through a Breather Break and is guided through the basic stress-reduction process that begins the Break, that person gets better at the process. Learning takes place. After a few weeks of daily guidance, the process begins to become automatic – and a major advancement has been accomplished in minimizing stress and mental fatigue, and maximizing clear conscious mental focus at work.

This is why Breather Breaks are scheduled 4 times a day, day in and day out, for six weeks – and often continued as a basic routine indefinitely into the future. The intent is to develop a permanent new habit that serves both employee and employer equally. And steady reinforcement is needed to meet that goal.

Also of key importance, throughout, is the mutual agreement that zero manipulation be involved in this approach to at-work mental-emotional training and support. The aim is not

further conditioning – the aim is to progressively set each of your employees free from old negative focal habits that interfere with that person's enjoyment of life, wellness, and successful performance in your company.

Transformation … or Discovery?

Currently there is much talk about completely transforming companies from the top-down. This notion of instigating radical change throughout an organization is appealing – but the hard truth is that most employees are already feeling overwhelmed with the demands of too much over-rapid change in their lives.

- In this light we prefer to talk about discovery instead of transformation. Rather than threatening to provoke any abrupt psychological or environmental change, we offer to help employees discover their inner pre-existing mental and emotional qualities that are currently lying mostly dormant, just awaiting the chance to rise up to the fore in positive expression.

This focus on 'discovering who we really are' rather than on 'trying to change who we are' lies at the heart of this new vision of tapping full employee potential. The aim is to help your employees discover and honor, and then realistically implement, their deeper pre-existing capacities.

This 'talent tap' goal can only be achieved if your employees regularly have the opportunity (and the needed guidance) to shift temporarily out of thinking-as-usual mode into a mindset where they quiet all the habitual mental chatter, tune into their deeper presence for a few breaths, and begin to discover for themselves their expanded potential for teamwork, innovation, and success.

In Sum

We began this chapter talking about the fact that your employees are your primary company asset. If you decide to explore and mine that asset to its fullest, via a process such as we're discussing here, you will find that you quite quickly unleash a greater flow of productivity and innovation throughout your workforce, matched by a heightened surge of employee motivation, and managed by a fine-tuned quality of focused attention that can step by conscious step expand and manifest your company vision.

The underlying aim of this new Breather Break/Focus Phrase strategy is to regularly immerse your employees in the 30 primary focus themes that predictably generate a movement toward optimum mental, physical, and emotional mindsets. The goal of inserting this higher mental stimulus into your company culture can be accomplished within a short time-frame and enjoyable format, and will steadily advance your organization into higher levels of wellness, innovation and accomplishment.

Part ONE:

Realistically, What Needs To Change?

Item 1: Reducing Psychological Stress

__Click Here to Watch Item 1 Video__

We all face the daily reality that work in America has become progressively (even sometimes exponentially) more stressful. At the same time for most employees, work has become less rewarding. Employees are required to do more at work and do it faster and longer – and the result? Their core vitality, their innovative spark, their mental performance and their team spirit are all being steadily undermined.

The at-work impact of too much mental tension and non-stop time pressure is well-documented: cognitive performance takes a dive, chronic fatigue erodes one's energetic stance, creative breakthroughs drop by the wayside, employee health and job-satisfaction continue to sink, errors in judgment happen more often – and enjoyment of life gets totally lost.

- Even though studies show that multitasking reduces cognitive acuity, that worrying generates negative performance, and that non-stop tension undermines our health, we seem stuck without mercy in stress mode.

Meanwhile a company's core asset – employee access to new insight and wise action – is being directly impaired, because stress reduces connectivity with breakthrough thinking.

At this point in time, chances are your organization has tried out various traditional stress-relief programs. Unfortunately, most of these programs focus on reducing the myriad symptoms, rather than the underlying cause, of stress – and thus have proven less than fully satisfactory, especially in the long term.

Also I'm sure you've attempted to change at least some of the obvious external stressors at work – but there will always be time pressure and performance demands, personal conflicts and emotional upsets, not to mention a plethora of other negative attention-grabbers, that in turn generate more frustration, confusion, misjudgment, hostility, depression and fatigue.

The problematic net result: Unhealthy mental and emotional stress remains solidly in place at work, damaging wellness and productivity alike. We continue to head off to work each morning feeling tense in anticipation of the negative ambiance that awaits us in the office – realistically, what can we do?

Treating stress per se will in fact always prove futile, because stress is merely a symptom of a deeper dilemma. We need to identify the primary cognitive and emotional generator of at-work stress – and then inject specific strategies into the work situation to actively reduce that causal fact.

As cognitive studies have fully documented, most stress is not created by external stressors – stress is an internal condition generated by how we respond to the situation we're in.

- As you've observed a great many times, two people can be in the exact same work situation – and yet one person reacts with high-stress confusion, agitation and fatigue while the other responds with creative low-stress wise action.

To make a long psychological explanation short, this is because those two people carry around in their heads and bodies quite different core attitudes and preconditioned emotional reactions related to the situation – therefore one dysfunctions while the other shines.

They are operating, as brain scans demonstrate, in entirely different regions of their brains – and focusing on entirely different dynamics of the situation. The result is that one is caught in high-stress while the other is functioning relatively free of stress.

- We see two key facts here. First, stress is determined by the way in which a person habitually manages his or her mind. Secondly, there's a choice present – to habitually focus upon stress-generating thoughts and reactions related to the situation; or to consciously re-focus on stress-reducing thoughts and perceptions.

Everyone brings to work each morning a whole host of potential moods and stances, emotions and attitudes. Which of these manifests during the workday will determine that employee's productivity and sense of fulfillment during that day. That's the reality of the situation.

Yes – chronic at-work stress is driving everyone quietly crazy. The key question is: how can everyone on your team learn to manage their own minds so that they focus attention regularly in directions that encourage the expression of moods and attitudes that further the whole-company success story?

Cognitive Shifting: Inserting Wisdom Into The Madness

Almost certainly you've already done your best to put together the best team you can. The issue is how to bring out the best in that team. The answer is found in the psychological process called cognitive shifting.

Cognitive shifting refers to the brain's automatic or conscious capacity to shift its focus of attention quickly from one mental mode to another.

Stick with me here a moment, let's understand this core mental process very clearly:

- Each and every moment at work, each employee is focusing his or her attention in a particular mental or perceptual direction.

- Shift that focus of attention, and you change everything.

- Shift that focus with clear positive intent and you predictably improve the functioning of that employee.

- Our discussion here is based solidly on this cognitive-shifting dynamic, because it's the most-clearly identified variable that everyone on your team can readily alter, in order to induce higher mental performance, brighter emotional presence, sharper intuitive insight, and lower-stress wellness.

In this discussion we're exploring an employee's inherent ability to employ cognitive shifting to move at will into what we call the WiZone – that special totally-aware quality of consciousness that athletes depend on for superior performance, and that employees likewise can tap into and reap the rewards thereof.

During the last decade we've demystified "being in the zone" so that it can be approached as a predictable at-work accomplishment, not just a mysterious out-of-the-blue athletic blessing. Even in the midst of the madness of stressed-out work, as we'll see, your team individually or en masse can choose to shift their attention away from habitual fixation on stressful reactions, toward an entirely different whole-brain mental mode – one that short-circuits the stress reaction and spurs empathy and insight.

- By regularly pausing and shifting into the WiZone at work, your team will be able to let go of stress, access more insightful realizations and decisions, which will in turn help them evolve their work experience in more rewarding directions.

How Is This Shifting Accomplished?

Once you understand the dynamics of intentional re-focusing, the mental act of shifting out of stress/contraction mode into relax/realize mode is straight-forward and easy for anyone to master. For instance, most psychological stress is generated by imagining a situation as potentially dangerous in the future.

- Time pressure, as an example, is just that – it's the apprehension that there won't be enough time left to get a job done right, and therefore something bad is probably going to happen.

Universally, time pressure is a primary stressor. Often a deadline is even arbitrarily set up – but then people begin to act as if the world will end if the deadline is missed. Thus even fairly unimportant deadlines can generate a physiological (and often unconscious) stress reaction of life-or-death emotions that can infect an entire company, reducing present-moment performance and in fact slowing work down rather than speeding it up.

Whenever you're holding even a vague apprehension in the back of your mind about a possible negative development in the future, you're in stress – because you're worried that something negative might perhaps happen.

The usual reaction to a perceived future problem or threat is to shift into agitated problem-solving – and indeed far too much problem-solving is driven by stressed apprehensive emotions which then cloud and impede successful thinking.

- A certain amount of stress is of course good for a person's performance; we often need a bit of provocation in order to shift into high gear. But very soon that initial rush of energy turns into manic mental activity that often gets nothing done fast.

Temporary present-moment stress induced by an immediate threat to one's well-being (a lion attacking, a bus coming at you in the street) elicits a fear-reaction that charges your system to prepare to fight or run for it – action! But most stressful situations at work aren't short term, they're upsetting anticipations and mental projections into a possible negative future that you can't run away from or fight because, well ... the imagined danger is still just an imagination.

Meanwhile the perceived stress situation will provoke more and more hurrying and speedy mental gymnastics as the manic brain and stressed body, loaded with fight-or-flight stress hormones (fight or flight), exhausts itself.

There was an old adage in the sixties that said "Speed kills – take it easy." Stress is definitely synonymous with chronic hurrying. And cognitive studies show that the brain cannot run overlong with such manic buzzing thoughts before it begins to malfunction – resulting in burn-out and poor performance.

The hurry problem is exacerbated by the universal habit of trying to second-guess the future, in order to be prepared just in case the very worst possible future scenario of a situation happens. Many executives and managers actually believe they're not really doing their job if they're not constantly worrying about what might go wrong.

- To a certain extent this is often called for – but in most cases, bothersome and even mentally-debilitating stress is generated by too much worrying about the future. The result is lowered judgment, faulty communication, and the generation of problems, not the avoidance of them.

When stress grips a leader or an employee, and performance, judgment, and empathy begin dropping by the wayside, what's to be done? The wise move is to temporarily shift one's inner focus of attention away from all worried hurried thoughts and apprehensions that are gripping the mind, breath and body … and to re-focus in present-moment directions that generate inner calm, clarity, balance and insight.

In order to almost instantly achieve this goal, studies show that the optimum thing to refocus attention on is a distinct present-moment sensation in the body.

- This shifting process is accomplished most effectively when a person is able to pause momentarily from work to temporarily quiet the entire buzz of problem-solving thoughts and tense emotions, and tune into physical bodily sensations.

Why this sensation focus? Back in my early research years, I participated in a primary research study in perceptual research for NIH that showed that when a person focuses attention on two or more sensory inputs at the same time, all thoughts temporarily stop, as evidenced in EEG and brain-scan research.

Since then, my colleagues and I have been evolving more and more effective ways for employees learn how to attain mental silence. The fastest technique is to have them turn their focus of attention first toward the sensation of the air they're breathing, using the Focus Phrase:

"I feel the air flowing in and out of my nose ..."

Then they are instructed to expand their focus to also include the breath sensations down in their torso:

"I also feel the movements in my chest and belly as I breathe."

These powerful refocusing statements aim their attention directly toward many sensations at once – which in turn predictably and effortlessly quiets the flow of thoughts through their minds, and thus sets them free from the mental content that was generating their stress condition.

Focus On Enjoying The Moment

Stress is no fun – enjoyment of the present moment gets entirely lost when we focus anxiously on possible future problems or disasters, and overall performance at work also deteriorates when we're not enjoying ourselves. There's another Focus Phrase that almost instantly helps an employee shift his or her attention away from judgmental or worried fixations, toward present-moment enjoyment and participation – let's consider it for a moment.

If our intent is to shift instantly away from upsetting and judgmental thoughts, toward feeling good and energized in the present moment, then an optimum Focus Phrase would be expressed with these words:

"I choose to enjoy this moment."

Just by bringing this short thought to mind, an employee immediately entertains the possibility of shifting in this positive direction. "Say it – do it," is the psychological motto for this type of process. Conscious awareness of a choice initiates the choice itself – and who doesn't want to enjoy this moment? Nothing negative happens to a company when employees choose to feel good – and an array of beneficial things happen.

If just one person on your team is holding this focus phrase in mind privately throughout the day, there will certainly be an inner result of value: the mind will respond by realizing first of all that there is a choice in the present moment to focus on negative stressors, or to focus in positive directions that elicit a heightened sense of enjoyment. And – stress will predictably fall away quite rapidly when a person shifts from future worries toward a focus on positive inner and external present-moment experience.

- With no one else on the team regularly making this positive inner shift, the solitary practitioner of the focus phrase will be just one struggling bright light in an otherwise relatively-dark emotional environment – and we all know now easy it is to get pulled down into negative fixations when everyone else is stuck there.

However, when other people on a team are also holding in mind a focus phrase such as "I choose to enjoy this moment," suddenly there's powerful group-reinforcement dynamics at play. Just the experience of two people passing in the hallway and meeting each other's eyes can be of great impact, as they acknowledge that the other is also holding "I choose to enjoy this moment," in the back of their mind at the same time. They might smile at the shared realization – or stop and chat a moment about how they're doing with the focus phrase.

Two or more people focused on the same theme or intent will reinforce each other and augment the effectiveness of the theme or intent. And a whole company holding the same focal statement in mind will actively radiate with the creative resonance of that statement of intent.

"I choose to enjoy this moment."

Imagine for a whole day your whole company voluntarily holding this focus phrase in mind – what would be the emotional and behavioral impact?

Happiness Equals Productivity

The experience of shifting out of stress mode into whole-body presence almost always feels good – it's a relief! As stress goes down at work, enjoyment goes up, they're in a direct inverse proportion to each other, as many studies have shown.

- A recent study (see appendix for all research) found that "People who were happiest at work were 47% more productive than their least-happy colleagues. And they were productively contributing a day and a quarter more than their least-happy colleagues per week."

Another study demonstrated that employees in the highest happiness-rating group of a company had 180% more available energy than those who felt most unhappy at work. Furthermore in the same study, on the key 'engagement scale' the happiest employees felt 108% more engaged than their least happy colleagues, and they reported 82% more job satisfaction.

Reducing stress also directly induces innovation. As we'll explore in more depth later, chronic fixation on deductive problem-solving or detail thinking, especially when it generates stress, is not at all conducive to the kind of breakthrough thinking that generates insight and innovation in a company.

Intuitive flashes emerge from an entirely different function of the mind than deductive thinking, worrying, problem-solving, etc. Therefore only when the mind shifts temporarily out of think-think stress mode, can insights pop into mind.

The process of cognitive shifting that we're exploring here is the essential first step toward awakening an innovative flash of insight at work – because the habitual thinking mind must temporarily become silent, in order to allow flashes of wisdom and insight to suddenly emerge. This is why allowing employees to regularly pause for a Breather Break opens up the potential for sudden insight – this is very important to a company, and we'll explore the theme further later on in this discussion.

Employee Satisfaction

Even though many Americans are out of work, companies continue to struggle to keep top-notch employees on the payroll. Everyone these days wants to find work that is less stressful or even actually good for their health; they want to feel that their employer cares for them; they want to feel valued not just for the grunt work but for their creative insights; and they want a work environment that is positive, friendly, even fun at times.

Using cognitive shifting and Focus Phrase technologies, everyone on your team can learn to regularly break free from unhealthy stress – and thus improve their morale, their health, their innovation and their productivity.

Another billboard from times gone by said "Slow down and live." It was meant for speedy drivers but today it applies equally to speedy thinkers. In this age of super computers the truth is, we can't think as fast as our computers can – but we seem to be determined to die trying.

Perhaps you remember the Charlie Chaplin movie where he's working in a factory and the machines keep going faster and faster and he keeps trying to speed up faster and faster to keep up with the machines – finally with totally disastrous results.

We're at that stage right now in almost every office building in the country – everyone's running faster and faster, but in reality the brain has its limits that ultimately, when violated, lead to breakdown in performance. Manic brain work often ends up as throwaway work.

- There's nothing worse than an employee who's driven by manic stress who starts making poor decisions and multiple errors without even realizing it, and meanwhile is so lost in thoughts about a pressing future that he falters in the present moment, fails to recognize problems staring him in the face, and furthermore upsets everyone around him because of his manic heartless behavior.

Regular Breather Breaks inserted into a busy workday are designed to enable employees to regain their senses, recover their composure, remember they're human, and return to work more centered, responsible, and happy.

A general rule of thumb that we encourage is this:

When you catch yourself going too fast, when you're lost in stressful thoughts, out of touch with your emotions and bodily presence, and in general buzzing too fast to maintain your equilibrium and clarity and sense of purpose at work, it's time to pause, let the dust settle – and then return to your work, but at maybe a 10% slower speed than you were buzzing at when you started to burn out.

Human beings do have realistic biological limits, and chronic stress drives us beyond those limits. For the sake of everyone involved, including one's company as a whole, it's wise to slow down enough at work so that stress doesn't generate progressive malfunctioning.

- In redefining work, this is a vital new concept – slow down and get real. Ease up and get better results. Speed kills – take it easy.

Stress And America's Future

As we explore how to help employees shift their focus of attention so as to regain their senses and reclaim their souls at work, we are definitely advancing a new notion of what work in America can aspire toward.

- By adopting and teaching wiser (i.e. more efficient, healthy, and innovative) focus habits at work, American companies can actively raise our economy up by the bootstraps and move us back into prominence as the leader – with new in-house approaches to maximizing productivity, creativity, and worker satisfaction.

While the rest of the world continues to try to mimic computer-pace thinking (and run themselves dangerously over a cliff stress-wise in the process) we can advance into a new approach to work where we stop believing that speed is everything, and realize that clarity, insight, wisdom, and whole-body participation at work are our leading qualities for nurturing inspired breakthroughs and long-term success.

Hold in mind however, that ingrained stress-driven focus habits take time to evolve in positive directions – realistically there is no magic quick-fix for raising the overall quality of health, performance, and innovation in the workplace. Transforming work will require a solid long-term approach involving daily training and reinforcement paradigms.

The at-work insertion programs we're recommending are structured to immerse employees in a long-term process that understands how realistic change takes place, and works in small daily steps to teach a seriously-new way of making choices and shifting focus in rewarding directions.

Item 2: Lowering Health Costs

__Click Here to Watch Item 2 Video__

We all know the dire straits we're in health-wise. Without reform, annual per employee health care costs for American companies will triple to nearly $29,000 by 2019 according to a report commissioned by the Business Roundtable, an association of chief executive officers of leading US companies.

The United States spends an estimated $2 trillion annually on health care expenses, more than any other industrialized country.

- According to data from the Organization for Economic Cooperation and Development (OECD), the United States spends two-and-a-half times more than the OECD average: Americans consumed $7,290 of health services per person in 2007, almost two-and-a-half times more than the OECD average of just under $3,000. Americans spend more than twice as much as relatively rich European countries such as France, Germany and the United Kingdom. The OECD says the United States spent 16% of its national income (GDP) on health this year.

A recent Hewitt Associates report projects average health care cost per American employee will rise to $9,821 in 2011, up from $9,028 in 2010. Hewitt's report projects an 8.8 percent average increase in health insurance premiums for employers, compared to a 6.9 percent rise in 2010. Health care premiums will have more than doubled since 2001, from $4,083 to $9,821 in 2011.

The problem's obvious; premiums are too high. What can be done about this within the scope of the WizeWell Process? Plenty, when we take into account the high percentage of medical costs that are caused by stress and other emotional/ mental conditions that can be relieved through programs such as WizeWell.

Again, chronic stress at work is the variable that we can attack and reduce through insertion strategies. Consider these facts:

A 20-year study by the University College London found that unmanaged reactions to stress were a more dangerous risk factor for cancer and heart disease than either cigarette smoking or high-cholesterol foods. According to a study at Rockefeller University in New York City, stress can shrink brain cells, prematurely age the immune system, and disturb memory, decision making, and focus of attention functions.

- Likewise the Mayo Clinic concluded that acute and chronic stress can provoke a great many medical ailments including: stomach aches, diarrhea, weight gain, immune system breakdown, susceptibility to infections, depression, anxiety, sleep disturbances, loss of sex drive, eating disorders, hypertension, cholesterol issues, heart disease, stroke, skin conditions (psoriasis, eczema, hives, and acne), asthma attacks …

The list goes on and on, and each of these psychosomatic conditions leads predictably to a medical office visit, treatment, prescriptions, and higher health costs.

At the financial level, according to a 2006 study by HR.com, a Web site devoted to human resources issues, stress costs

U.S. businesses more than $300 billion annually. And note that that number has doubled in 10 years – this is a giant indicator.

Healthcare studies estimate that unmanaged at-work stress accounts for 40 percent of employee turnover; and half of the 550 million working days lost each year in the United States from absenteeism are stress related.

- In a recent American Psychological Association poll, one in four people said they have taken a "mental health day" due to work-related stress.

Another part of the problem with stress is that it contributes to poor lifestyle choices. A recent poll of 2,200 British working men found that one-third used alcohol to combat stress. Not getting enough sleep or exercise, and an accompanying weight gain, are other reactions that hamper a person's ability to manage stress.

Unfortunately there is still a stigma associated with admitting to being "stressed out." To get ahead, employees work longer and harder, and try not to let their boss or colleagues know if they are having a difficult time.

- Men with chronic work stress are nearly twice as likely as women to develop metabolic syndrome (abnormal cholesterol levels, increased blood pressure, elevated insulin levels, excess body fat around the waist), a precursor to coronary disease.

Behavioral conditions such as excessive irritability, trouble getting along with others, turning projects in late, having a hard time concentrating and grasping what they're supposed to do – these can all be attributed to poor coping strategies to stress.

Health-Cost Relief Strategy

Obviously a certain proportion of health conditions are genetic or accidental and cannot be avoided through behavioral and psychological interventions – but as we've seen, at least 50% of health costs are psychosomatic in origin, which means that we can use mind management to avoid the condition and cost.

Let me guide you through the logic that we are working with in this program, which shows a basic strategy required in order to directly impact employee health costs. Here's the logic flow:

- To reduce health costs and insurance premiums, visits to the doctor and medication costs must be lowered;

- To reduce visits to the doctor by perhaps 20-30%, psychological stress must be consistently lowered;

- To reduce at-work stress syndromes, employees must learn to consciously manage their focus of attention so as to shift out of habitual stress states in the mind, and focus on positive present-moment experiences.

- To accomplish this, employees must be given short breaks so they can self-manage their stress condition.

That's the strategy we're offering. The question is this – is your company willing to grant your employees three minutes four times a day, twelve minutes in total, so that they can pause regularly and self-manage their health profile in healthy directions?

Dee Edington in *Health As A Serious Economic Strategy*, states the case for at-work proactive health intervention this way: "The cost of waiting for people to get sick far exceeds the cost of helping healthy people stay healthy. No company will be successful in a globally competitive world with anything but healthy and productive people."

Emotional First Aid

Our program is not an instant cure for unhealthy stress – there is no such thing as instant change in this regard; however, each day of the initial 6-week process will advance your entire workforce in the direction of higher wellness and lower medical costs. You can also continue long-term with the program as a permanent dimension of your company atmosphere, adding new health inputs periodically.

For instance we will be teaching, along with the 30 core Focus Phrases, a powerful 1-minute Emotional First Aid process that anyone can use anytime, when they need to directly relieve the primary symptoms of stress – tight shallow breathing, combined with an upsetting fixation on stressful thoughts, plus bothersome dizziness or mental confusion.

The Emotional First Aid process also helps greatly with anxiety in general, and in breaking out of fatigue syndromes. When used regularly in your company, this one-minute 'breath intervention' process can be a life-saver on many levels:

- It will reduce the physical symptoms of stress by relaxing and deepening the breathing; it will also bring more oxygen to the brain and thus generate clear thinking and higher awareness;

- It will shift the person's attention into whole-body presence, to boost charisma and empathy, and vitality in general.

- It will provide a shift in consciousness emotionally from distressed, anxious, thoughts and emotions, toward bright present-moment feelings of enjoyment and inner balance.

The Emotional First Aid process is based on solid 'mindfulness' research (see a number of related medical papers at the end of this book) that verify the impact of this type of refocusing technique for recovery of healthy breathing and mental mindsets. It's simple and short enough to remember even in the most stressful situations, and builds on the first week's training.

With each inhale and exhale for 3 in-out breath cycles, a stressed person says silently the following words to themselves:

1: On your next **inhale** say the word *"I ..."* (this shifts your focus directly to your own presence)

2: On you next **exhale**, silently say the word *"am..."* (this verb awakens a sense of personal action)

3: On the next **inhale** say, *"here..."* (to further focus on the present moment)

4: On the next **exhale**, say *"now..."* (to shift from past-future fixations, directly into the here and now)

5: On the next **inhale**, say *"breathing..."* (to wake up deeper breathing, and reduces stress)

6: On the next **exhale**, say *"freely..."* (to fully set the breathing free of tense shallow stress-patterns – *more of the science on this later*)

To be effective, such verbal inserts must be short, and directly aimed at shifting focus in helpful directions. After a bit of practice, employees will quickly master this short process for refocusing away from negative feelings and thoughts, toward immediate rejuvenation of whole-body presence and power.

"I / am ... here / now ... breathing / freely ..."

Note: During the last 40 years, behavioral and cognitive-therapy research has fully documented the power of having a client hold particular positive one-liner statements in his or her mind, sometimes for a whole day, or indeed for an entire week between therapy sessions. We're adapting this proven psychological technology to a very specific purpose here – that of impacting the primary physiological expression of stress: tense shallow uneven breathing.

When this Emotional First Aid method is combined with the 30 Focus Phrases of the WizeWell Process, a solid intervention system begins to take effect, growing with each day and each new Focus Phrase being introduced. If you take a look at the WizeWell Guidebook which takes you through each day, you'll see clearly the pragmatic design of the process.

Part Of A Greater Whole

As my colleague Heidi Hanna documents in her book *SHARP: Simple Strategies To Boost Your Brainpower*, one of the prime indicators of a healthy employee is the positive feeling of being a valued member of a supporting social network. For many people, their work community is an important part of that social network.

The feeling of 'belonging to the same tribe' has been proven to reinforce health. This feeling emerges when people feel that they share common values and goals, interests and experiences. This 'safe feeling of togetherness' at both physical and mental levels directly reduces stress and boosts wellness, as is now well documented.

With the WizeWell Process, we are aiming to stimulate this deeper sense of shared supportive experience both through the universal Focus Phrases themselves, and through the special delivery system and schedule where everyone on the team focuses attention in the same direction on the same day, and has ample opportunity to talk about the theme of the day with fellow team members.

- Because the Focus Phrase themes often touch heart-felt ideas and emotions, the sense of team bonding goes especially deep, establishing relationships that are the emotional glue that holds companies together.

For instance, we introduce the following three 'interactive' community-togetherness Focus Phrases during our 6-week training;

"I am a good listener."

"I accept everyone I work with, just as they are."

"I choose to participate in trust, joy, and harmony."

Traditionally, employees on their own had to steal a bit of time here and there to try and self-manage their stress and wellness. With the insertion of the WizeWell Process into your company community routine, your employees' sense of community wellbeing becomes much greater. By your act of purposefully allowing both time and training for maximizing shared happiness at work, you augment the underlying health benefits. Happiness is one thing – sharing happiness is even better.

From Worried ... To Courageous

Obviously there will always be struggle and stress at work, and a certain level of struggle is good, as it provokes the feeling of meeting a challenge with courage and winning over that challenge.

Our intent isn't to eliminate stress and challenge in the workplace – it's to help people respond to it in a winning way. Thus the twelfth Focus Phrase of the program:

"I am ready to act with courage and integrity."

The opposite of courage is anxiety – and anxiety in one form or another, as we've seen, is behind most psychological stress, and is likewise the prime eroding enemy of health in general. So since the opposite of anxiety is courage, we purposefully aim an employee's attention and intent in the defined positive direction, so as to specifically over-ride the negative.

- That's the primary intent of behavioral and cognitive therapy – to override an ingrained negative attitude or belief with a new positive stance in life.

This tactic is the optimum approach, as we understand the situation, for using transparent psychological intervention to induce better health in the workplace.

As another example of a health-focused Focus Phrase, here's one that points attention clearly in desired directions – and as a person says and holds this statement of intent in mind, an inner positive growth is regularly stimulated:

"I feel safe, confident, and valued on my team."

Imagine everyone on your team holding this intent in mind for an entire day, and perhaps talking together about it here and there ... that's the power of Focus Phrases at the company level – to bring shared focus of attention directly to bear on key themes that underlie the health and success of your team as a whole.

De-Stress Applications

Most of us have key points during our workday that generate apprehensive contractions in our breathing, and in general make us feel stressed and anxious whether we admit this openly or not.

- Many people stress out just before a meeting, and suffer accordingly during the meeting because of reduced clarity, charisma, and compassion. Stress is also often felt as a deadline approaches. Scheduled encounters with superiors often provoke rising stress levels. Awaiting anyone or any situation that's new and unpredictable will generate anxiety and stress.

- Many employees get tense every time they approach their workplace. The anticipation of any situation or person associated with past emotional conflict or trauma can set off a stress reaction.

Each of these stress-provoking situations will erode an employee's long-term health profile. People need a specific process to apply to such stressor moments.

Right when they feel their breathing getting tight and shallow, their mind going foggy, their head feeling dizzy, their stomach tensing with anxiety, their charisma ebbing and their sense of personal power and presence disappearing – right at that moment, or even just before, they need to 'remember to remember' to bring a Focus Phrase to mind that will generate a positive shift in focus.

For instance, as we've seen, the Emotional First Aid statement can be used to great advantage: "I am … here now … breathing freely …" Other Focus Phrases that will work very well include:

"I let go of all my stress and worries, and feel peaceful inside."

"My mind is quiet – I feel calm and connected."

"I trust my spontaneous thoughts and expressions."

"I feel connected with my creative source."

What we're seeing here is the special dynamic clarified in cognitive therapy methodologies – that when negative emotions grab hold, it's necessary to fight fire with fire, to replace old fear-based one-liners with new positive statements that are realistic, authentic, and possible. And once again – practice makes perfect. Employees must get familiar with these Focus Phrases, in order to employ them effectively.

In this light, our delivery and reinforcement systems will prove invaluable. Rather than employees being dependent on their memories (which become temporarily faulty at just the wrong times) we provide computer and mobile access to instant audio and video support to help guide people through the needed process, right when it's most needed.

Choosing To Be Happy And Healthy

Most people feel that they're victims of their health conditions. But a great deal of recent research documents that we have remarkable control over our health destiny, if we manage our minds and thoughts properly. This doesn't mean discipline the mind to think only positive thoughts, and to run away from bad feelings. It means becoming more aware of all the thoughts that habitually run through the mind, and choosing as a general rule to focus in directions that make us feel good, rather than bad.

- Furthermore, studies show that we have the choice either to dwell overmuch on upsetting past and future memories and apprehensions, or to maintain a steady awareness focus in the here and now.

- We can't change the past nor enter the future and impact it – but we can definitely influence how we feel and act in the present moment. Here and now is the best focus of attention for running our lives in a positive manner – this is what we teach in the WizeWell Process.

The relatively-new division of psychological research and therapy called Positive Psychology aims specifically at this goal of helping people simply to feel happier in life – because multiple positive effects are generated at health and performance levels based on happiness levels.

In this spirit, we begin our WizeWell Process, as noted before, with the positive Focus Phrase:

"I choose to enjoy this moment."

This isn't just a wishy-washy positive affirmation – it aims a person's attention in a realistic direction they already know experientially, but have temporarily forgotten to focus on.

It's important that Focus Phrases be realistic, grounded in the laws of both pragmatism and cognitive science, aiming attention not toward lofty dreams and imaginations, but toward an immediately-attainable inner goal or experience.

What most people do seek in life is happiness, fulfillment, peace, pleasure and contentment. There is now considerable evidence proving what we all know to be true – that people who feel good and content are more successful, healthy and fulfilled than people who feel bad or unsatisfied most of the time. In their article "The Benefits of Frequent Positive Affect: Does Happiness Lead to Success?", Lyubomirsky et al. summarize recent research findings:

> "The cross-sectional evidence reveals that happy workers enjoy multiple advantages over their less happy peers. Individuals high in subjective well-being are more likely to 1) secure job interviews, 2) be evaluated more positively by supervisors once they obtain a job, 3) show superior performance and productivity, and 4) handle managerial jobs better. They are also 5) less likely to show counter-productive workplace behavior and job burnout."

The key term here is 'subjective wellbeing,' where an employee perceives her or himself as being happy and content at work.

The overall intent of the WizeWell program is to offer, on a daily basis, a positive opportunity and specific process for shifting regularly in the direction of feeling relaxed and good, rather than feeling stressed and bad. This is the mega-strategy for proactively boosting wellness at work – and of course, employees take their increased brightness and wellness home with them to enjoy with their friends and families.

The final 30th Focus Phrase of the program states this intent perfectly:

"I choose to feel calm, bright, healthy, and whole."

Everyone wants this inner feeling on a regular basis, even at work – but if they never focus in that direction during the workday, chances are they won't experience it.

- In this light, the WizeWell Process is perhaps best seen as a 'remember to remember' reinforcement program that, over and over again, reminds employees to remember their higher purpose and intent – to go through the workday being both productive, and at the same time enjoying the process of being productive. That's the optimum formula for both low health-costs and high success.

Item 3: Maximizing Productive Focus

Click Here to Watch Item 3 Video

When push comes to pull, each and every employee in your company has been hired to perform exactly the same task – their job definition is to fully put aside their personal interests during each workday, and focus their concerted power of attention creatively, devotedly, and productively upon whatever work needs doing in the company at any given moment. Their success in consistently focusing their mind's attention on company business will, to a great extent, determine the ongoing survival and advancement of your company.

Upon close examination, the most important asset your company possesses and manages is the combined focus of attention of each and every one of your employees. And there's no question: how employee attention is managed directly and impressively impacts productivity.

Because it's like water to fish, people often remain unaware of the primal dynamic of focused attention at work. But really, the key freedom that everyone possesses is her or his power to aim their personal attention each new moment wherever they so choose. What each of us focuses on determines what we get in life, so how we manage our focus of attention each emerging moment is crucial both to survival and personal fulfillment.

- Wise decisions emerge personally and business-wise when people begin to make more conscious choices, that truly serve them and their company, regarding where they focus their attention each new moment.

In this light, note that imbedded and implied in the formal definition of work (and the contract employees sign with their company) is the understanding that the employee is agreeing to regularly and effectively focus his or her attention wherever required by supervisor or job description.

- Even if you're the CEO of your company, you have basically leased your personal focus of attention to your employer during work hours (and often after work hours as well) – that's the primary agreement, even if it's not directly stated.

Following that logic, an employee's entire work experience will be continually determined by where they (habitually or consciously) choose to aim their power of attention. Everything that they accomplish each day will be based on how well they managed their <u>focused innovative expression</u>.

A person's underlying quality of life itself is continually being generated by what they choose to focus on. In fact the better half of wisdom is continually caught up in this core issue:

"What would it be wise to focus on, right now?"

When employees habitually mismanage or out and out waste their focus of attention, taking their eyes off the ball at work, or perhaps fixating overmuch on detail and failing to pause and evaluate the broader picture, they predictably miss their chance for greater success, and certainly reduce their productivity and value to the company.

Conversely, as people learn to master the fine art of focusing their attention in directions that further their higher intent, they optimize their performance and also their deeper sense of job satisfaction.

That said, one's company does lease its employees' focus of attention at work – but most of the time the employee carries moment-to-moment responsibility for deciding what to focus on, based on their general job description.

- For instance, most job descriptions imply that employees shall manage their focus of attention so that they don't get sucked overmuch into stress mode; therefore employees ultimately have the responsibility to learn how to run their own minds wisely – in fact they're being paid to do so.

In this light, how will the regular insertion of key Focus Phrases into the workday impact productivity? To answer this, first let's lay out several core psychological realizations that underlie the entire dynamic of the WizeWell Process.

It's important to know that there are four very different directions a person can aim their focus of attention; attaining a balance among these four focal targets is crucial both to productivity and to wellness, satisfaction, and enjoyment at work.

We can …

1: Focus on perception (present-moment sensations)

2: Focus on emotion (feelings and moods)

3: Focus on cognition (deductive thinking)

4: Focus on insight (whole-brain integration)

In the same way that our bodies organically know how to naturally maintain a healthy balance (homeostasis) of oxygen and carbon dioxide in our lungs plus a healthy balance of salt and sugar and other essential ingredients in our hemoglobin plus properly-modulated blood pressure and hormonal secretions and all the rest ... our body also knows how to maintain a healthy balance between thinking abstract past-future thoughts, perceiving present-moment bodily experience, experiencing inner emotional flows and pressures, and tapping the inflow of creative insight.

When the mind fixates over-long on past-future thinking, numbers-crunching, rapid computer busyness and other abstract mental work, it's proven that performance drops, errors increase, satisfaction crashes, and overall health is negatively impacted.

- The stress reaction, when analyzed from this wider perspective of inner mental balance, is generated when we fixate overmuch and overlong on difficult mental activity in our brain, and under-fixate on our present-moment physical and emotional experience.

When we push ourselves too fast for too long with too much thinking about details, the result is that we lose awareness of our own bodies, of our breathing, of the pleasure of movement, and especially of our emotional feelings.

- Stated bluntly, during chronic work-stress we become bio-robots that have temporarily lost that essential four-way inner balance that makes us human, that makes us creative and empathic, that makes us feel good and happy and fulfilled at work.

As you might guess from reading this far into this discussion, the optimal solution to this chronic stress-generated focal imbalance is to regularly pause and regain our senses – to purposefully shift focus away from multi-tasking and point-fixation on details, so that we can reconnect with our physical and emotional selves, and tap into our deeper wellsprings of creative healthy expression at work.

The cognitive-shifting programs being explored in this book demonstrate how this at-work focal homeostasis can be readily achieved, to everyone's advantage.

Focus Phrase Power

Ever since the birth of cognitive science in the 1960s, remarkable advancements have emerged regarding how the mind orchestrates emotional and physical balance, and how we can actively insert breather breaks and cognitive-refocusing phrases into the workplace to restore inner balance when that balance has been lost.

At the core of cognitive psychology and behavioral therapy is in fact the use of focal statements – a sentence that is brought to mind regularly, over time, to gently re-aim the mind's attention in more rewarding directions.

Recently, through the innovative work of a growing number of professors and professionals throughout the world and especially in America, cognitive science has made a new and highly-effective discovery also known for thousands of years in the meditative community:

One of the basic causes of burn-out, lowered productivity, chronic stress and mental and emotional imbalance is our society's general inability to periodically quiet the entire noisy chatter of our thinking minds. We're stuck all day long in cognitive mode.

Even though most of us highly value the fleeting experience of inner peace and quiet relaxation, and know deep-down that our own worry-fixated thoughts are generating most of our stress and unhappiness in our lives, we simply don't know how to 'just say no' to that non-stop chatter that fills the back of our minds with tension, confusion, turmoil, anxiety, depression and all of the negatives that reduce our performance and make life a living hell.

We're personally responsible for the thoughts that we think, the memories and apprehensions that we let dominate our minds – but we don't know how to take charge and actively quiet those thoughts.

- One of the long-term studies of the authors of this book has been to discover pragmatic techniques to quickly quiet the flow of thoughts through the mind on a regular basis, so that a bit of peace and clarity can be predictably inserted into the work experience.

Traditional meditation programs aim to silence the mind, but for most people these ancient methods are hard to master, as companies have found out when they've tried to insert meditation breaks into the workplace. Their lengthy time-frame is also counter-productive to getting a full day's work done.

But when we combine traditional meditative wisdom with the nuts-and-bolts insights of cognitive science, we can put together a sure-fire process for quickly and enjoyably quieting the mind of its stressful chatter.

Especially when using online video guidance and mobile-driven reinforcement, employees and executives alike can pause for just a couple of minutes periodically throughout the day – and employ specific Focus Phrases that immediately shift the focus of attention temporarily away from all the stress-generating internal busy-ness of problem-solving efforts, toward present-moment relief and recharging.

As people master this process, they reap more and more benefits of the short refresh-recharge experience that rebalances their energetic system and restores creativity, empathy, wellness, and endurance.

Easier Said Than Done?

The reason that there have been no programs to date that directly address the underlying cause of focal stress and all its debilitating symptoms is simple – we hadn't reached the point of clarity in cognitive research to enable us to see to the core of the dilemma, and thus generate logical solutions to the problem.

- We can now seriously redefine work based on new insights into how the mind malfunctions under stress at work – and develop cognitive technologies that regularly short-circuit the cause of stress and re-invigorate the mind to perform at higher levels.

And again, our inherent ability to refocus our power of attention whenever and wherever we want to provides the practical tool for getting the job done.

As mentioned before, this approach to reducing stress (and improving all the positives that make a company strong and successful) is not a short-term in-and-out type of program – it's

incremental. Once the first 6-week round is completed, the process spirals up through another 6-week round with the same Focus Phrases but new support material.

- Why the repetition? Because studies show clearly that

repetition is required in order for this deeper type of rebalancing to become permanent.

Our Focus Phrases have been carefully developed during the last decade to resonate so deeply that employees will eagerly look forward to refocusing on the 6 themes and 24 Focus Phrases well into the future, as the spiral effect continues to take the company higher.

What's important is that employees see the 4 short Breather Breaks each day as a gift from their employer – an opportunity to pause, regain their senses, recover from mental burn-out, and refresh the inner sense of enjoying the moment at work.

Traditionally, most employees in a manufacturing-based economy were hired to do robotic mechanical jobs with their physical bodies, demanding very little cognitive work. That has drastically changed in the last fifty years to where employees are more and more challenged to:

1: work non-stop with their thinking minds

2: assume more perspective and responsibility

3: be regularly affable and empathic

4: contribute innovative ideas and creative solutions

To meet this new 4-part definition of work, which requires all four types of focused attention, employees must be helped to shift rapidly from one mode to another, and to maintain an adequate charge of energy so that their focused attention has an impact.

The logical way to deliver this support and guidance is through using Focus Phrases and periodic Breather Breaks to make sure everyone is functioning at top performance.

Enjoyable Productivity

With all the recurrent economic downturns, work has turned more and more into a stressful negative burden on everyone. Yes, productivity has been maintained and even boosted in America thus far, but at a terrible and unsustainable human price. With stress now endemic and wellness under siege, innovation has steadily sagged, and employee satisfaction is at an all-time low.

If companies want to survive and even thrive during these hard times, they must pro-actively introduce into the workplace something more than palliative band-aid alterations in the physical workplace.

Companies must redefine work as an enjoyable productive experience where basic human needs are openly honored and addressed, and the underlying dynamics of cognitive science clearly adhered to.

- This is the only realistic solution to our stressed-out dilemma. Regardless of the prevailing economic upturn or downturn, we need to understand how to insert regular short refresh-recharge breaks into the everyday work experience, so that employees high and low have the freedom to focus temporarily in directions that predictably restore mental, physical and emotional homeostasis.

This is the wise approach to redefining work, because it's based both on common sense, scientific research, ancient wisdom, employee needs and business requirements.

Mental Flexibility For Top Performance

Another primary value of periodic breaks (during which employees pause and actively shift from one type of focused attention to another) is that this shifting process is regularly exercising that employee's mental flexibility in cognitive shifting. The ability to shift rapidly between the four modes of mental activity is key to a highly-productive team.

- Just like a physical muscle, the mind needs practice, repetition, and focused exercise in order to remain in top performance. The four daily Breather Breaks we're recommending in the WizeWell Process are just that – exercise breaks that allow the mental muscle to shift, relax, re-tune, and recover.

By pausing to relax and stretch the mind, to throw off tensions and encourage present-moment enjoyment in the mental muscle, an employee quickly overcomes the mental spasm of stress, and prepares for reentry into work with a mind prepped for top performance.

Even without the positive guidance we offer, new productivity research just completed at the University of Copenhagen showed that employees who were allowed a short distraction before completing a task had significantly fewer errors while doing the task than the control group that wasn't allowed the break.

- The classic 'cookie study' also demonstrated without question that when people are offered a short positive experience (in the study it was getting to eat a cookie) before doing a hard mental task, they perform at higher levels than the control group that didn't get a cookie.

If short distractions and cookies can boost performance, periodic positive experience and cognitive re-focusing exercises will do even more, when well-managed and properly timed.

Employee Performance Re-Envisioned

The human brain is the primary instrument that determines employee performance, no one argues that. So what does that 3-pound grey-matter organ in the cranium need in order to perform at optimum levels?

a) First of all, the brain requires proper oxygen/CO_2 levels in the blood reaching the brain – and stress directly disturbs optimum oxygen/CO_2 levels in the brain, thus lowering brain function in general.

b) At another level, the brain requires a harmonious positive emotional condition in the body, in order to think clearly, make rational decisions, access wisdom and insight, and communicate clearly and fairly – when emotions turn negative and get out of control, the brain malfunctions and performs terribly.

c) In order to perceive a situation at work objectively, and respond realistically, the brain needs reality-based attitudes, opinions, and beliefs that process situations that develop, and allow for reasonable decisions and actions – but all too often, employees carry around out-dated attitudes and assumptions that directly thwart realistic positive decisions and actions.

d) To orchestrate production at optimum levels, the brain needs a solid shared set of values and goals that resonate with the company vision – but in many cases, employees carry old distorted values and goals that offer resistance rather than reinforcement of company values and goals.

e) Perhaps most important, in order to accomplish work and produce goods and services of value, the brain requires a set of <u>focusing habits and directives</u> that ensure consistent, effective, and enduring focus of attention where most needed at work.

In re-visioning work in America, we need to address these five primary needs of the human brain, in order for it to orchestrate all the various mental, emotional and physical actions that in turn generate the products and services that companies are aiming to deliver to the marketplace. As this discussion intends to present, the WizeWell Process is an integrative method for achieving all five of these core brain-needs in one concise cognitive technology.

- In reality, all five of these brain requirements are inseparable – they're working together at bio-chemical, emotional, physical and cognitive levels to influence the final behavioral outcome.

Underlying the WizeWell strategy is the inescapable fact mentioned earlier that ultimately, executives and managers and coaches cannot force an employee to focus his or her attention anywhere at all. It's the privilege and freedom and responsibility of each employee to take charge of their focusing habits, and develop optimum focal strength, flexibility, and intent.

Only when the employee realizes that this focus-of-attention issue is a win-win enterprise, will companies succeed in working with their team members, on a daily basis, to develop new mental and emotional habits that ensure that employee focus of attention serves (at the same time) the needs of the company, and the needs of the employee.

Then we will have satisfied employees who eagerly work to meet company goals – with a minimum of stress, a maximum of creativity, and a unity of intent.

Item 4: Nurturing Innovation

Click Here to Watch Item 4 Video

There's so much fluff flying around about how to magically wake up creativity and boost innovation at work. Let's spend a few pages here getting serious about the reality of how the creative mind functions, and what procedures will most directly enable employees to access flashes of insight and breakthrough thinking on a regular basis.

- The authors of this book some time ago participated in whole-brain research with EEG brain-wave equipment; more recently, brain-scan technologies have given us a front-center full-color panorama of the brain's activity in different cognitive, behavioral, and perceptual modes of operation. Brain-mapping has become remarkably fine-tuned regarding which regions of the brain are active during particular mental functions.

It's quite clear that there's a dramatic difference between usual problem-solving numbers-crunching mental activity which takes place mostly in the left hemisphere of the brain, and sudden brain-storming intuitive flashes of insight that activate right-hemisphere activity, and more importantly integrate both hemispheres in a higher-order mental process.

Nowhere is this whole-brain aspect of cognitive activity more important than in the still-mysterious phenomenon we call creative or innovative thinking.

Indeed, even talking about 'innovative thinking' is misleading because right at the moment when a flash of creative insight happens in the brain, everyday deductive thinking is completely absent from the experience. Our normal stream of thoughts are linear in nature, moving through the mind one thought or phrase or image after another.

Most of the time we are locked into this linear flow of time – but the mind can also shift into an entirely different perception of time where the linear flow is replaced by the sudden experience of 'seeing the whole'.

Everyone now that then experiences this alternate process of experiencing time. Whenever we pause and momentarily 'get lost' in enjoying a sunset or some other esthetically-moving perceptual experience, we momentarily let go of normal linear mental functioning and 'see the whole' at once, as if we're 'out of time'.

- It's the same when we enjoy a great meal, or are transported by listening to music, or 'move into the zone' while jogging, or hopefully while making love … we are moved by a deeper experience than normal thinking, into a quality of consciousness that seems to wake up an immersive sense of participation in, and enjoyment of, the flow of life itself.

Here's the crucial point: our flashes of insight, those sudden breakthrough realizations and moments of seeing to the heart of a problem and perceiving its solution – indeed all of our creative experience seems to come to us when we are momentarily shifted into this very particular present-moment mode of consciousness.

When this universal but quite-skittish phenomenon of creative insight is scrutinized with the tools of cognitive science, one particular fact stands out: only when the habitual everyday flow of linear thoughts (the internal chatter that usually dominates our focus of attention) become momentarily quiet, and we shift 'into neutral' for a moment, does the creative muse we all seek actually speak to us from this temporary inner silence.

- Receiving and mining such 'out of the blue' creative insights is essential to long-term success. Companies rise or perish based on the frequency of whole-brain insights and creative breakthroughs in their workforce.

However, the innovative muse cannot be forced, it emerges spontaneously right when we least expect it – perhaps while taking a shower or walking along a hallway or driving to work.

The question is – how can we actively enable employees to regularly shift into this quiet receptive state of mind, so that insights are nourished, not habitually blocked and ignored?

At the end of this discussion, in the science section, you can read various studies that highlight this 'whole-brain quiet-mind creative phenomenon' related to innovation. What's key here is that the act of creation in the human mind is linked directly to the following process:

Stage One: **The Cognitive Fry** ~ An employee high or low has been busy, perhaps for hours or even days on end, struggling with a problem, crunching a myriad of details and still lost in the midst of a difficult dilemma or complex decision.

- When burn-out is approaching; confusion reigns; the linear point-by-point analytical function of the brain has done its best, but it not been able to generate an answer or resolution;

Stage Two: **The Cognitive Shift** ~ The employee realizes that it's time to shift out of deduction-mode into insight-mode – and knows that to do this, it's essential first to quiet the usual chatter and fixations of the mind, and enter into a temporary neutral zone where the thinking mind becomes quiet, and the present moment becomes all.

- The first week of the WizeWell Process teaches the most powerful method we've found for temporarily quieting the thinking mind, and shifting into total focus on present-moment experience – where the focus is on sensory perception, not analytical deduction.

As mentioned before, when a person focuses on two or more perceptual (sensory) inputs at the same time, all thoughts temporarily stop. Therefore we work in Week One with the following 4 Focus Phrases, one for each breath:

1: "I choose to enjoy this moment..." (this focus on enjoyment in the moment begins the quiet-mind shift);

2: "I feel the air flowing in and out of my nose..." (this shift to pure perception of an ongoing sensory event instantly changes brain activity from cognition to perception);

3: "I also feel the movements in my chest and belly as I breathe..." (the brain focuses on a great many sensations at once down in the torso, and all thoughts become quiet);

4: "I'm aware of my whole body at once, here in this present moment..." (this completes the cognitive shift from thinking, which is a past-future function of the mind, to experiencing, which is a present-moment perceptual function of the mind;

- After practicing this process, most employees will become quite good at making the quiet-mind present-moment shift – practice does make perfect, and our training system delivers adequate reinforcement.

We saw earlier that this first week of the WizeWell Process reduces psychological stress and thus improves long-term health. Here we see that, at exactly the same time, something equally important is being accomplished.

During a Breather Break, employees shift temporarily into a state of mind in which they are highly receptive to experiencing sudden "Aha!" flashes of insight, which then take concrete form as breakthrough thinking once the mind shifts back into normal thinking-mode.

- This is the required step in consciously optimizing the occurrence of creative insight and innovative vision. When an employee pauses for 3 minutes 4 times each workday and enters 'the creative zone' on company time, that company is purposefully tapping the universal font of new ideas and expanded vision.

Stage Three: **The Innovation Focus Phrase**

Insight and inspiration are spoken of as an inflow of brilliance into the thinking mind. The Latin root of inspiration, *in-spire*, means literally to inhale, showing the tight link-up between the inflow of air through the nose, and the inflow of creative ideas into the mind.

- As we'll see, all of the 18 Focus Phrases following the first week of WizeWell training require the initial focus on one's breath experience, for them to be activated.

Developing more-conscious breath awareness as a lifelong habit is indeed vital on many levels, because this ongoing awareness of the primary organic process that keeps us alive moment to moment also keeps us fully present and alert, grounded not only in our thoughts but also in our bodies, our emotions, perceptions, and our higher sense of creativity, wisdom and purpose.

With breath awareness and whole-body presence activated, an employee is now ideally prepared to bring to mind the 9th Focus Phrase, the Insight Phrase. By design it is quite short and utterly to the point:

"I am open to receive … insight and guidance."

Most of the time most employees are simply not open to receive insight – their minds are so caught up in detail work and past-future ruminations that they never even approach a quiet-mind present-moment mode of consciousness where they are receptive to the inflow of innovative ideas.

Optimally, each employee needs scheduled 'insight time' to temporarily pause, quiet the mind and cool off their fried synapses … and then purposefully focus attention exactly in the direction where insight comes flowing effortlessly into the conscious mind. "I am open to receive…"

- Science doesn't pretend to understand how the creative act happens in the mind; brain scans only take us so far in this understanding … the mystery remains. But just like, for many years, we didn't really understand what electricity was but were still able to use it to great advantage, we don't have to fully grasp how and where and why innovative insights spring suddenly to mind, in order to tap and reap their benefits.

The way to optimize the occurrence of inspired ideas popping into the mind of every employee in your company is to openly provide paid time for that employee to perform a particular mental act that aims his or her inner attention directly toward the reception-point of insight and innovation.

I am open to receive …

Say … do it.

And what specifically is an employee opening his or her mind to receive during a breather Break?

… insight and guidance.

Note that in both the Christian, Buddhist, Hindu, Muslim, and Taoist traditions, this 'ask and receive' theme has been a cornerstone to human prayer and meditation. Jesus promised specifically, "Ask, and you shall receive." But if we don't ask, if we don't state our need and intention, chances are we won't be looking in the direction that the solution will come from.

I am open to receive insight …

The very act of holding these words in one's mind predisposes that person to be in position to recognize and receive insight into what is most pressing for breakthrough and resolution.

And remember the last line of our definition of wisdom?

"A synonym for wisdom is insight."

Wisdom is an integrative quality of consciousness where we quiet our usual detail mode of thinking and shift into a more expansive whole-brain modality where we can see the whole of a situation, receive insight into the situation, and then act accordingly.

Managing Insight

Different companies have different needs related to employee innovation. For some companies, just inserting this 9th Focus Phrase during Week Three will be enough to help move the company as a whole in this creative direction. Other companies will want a more regular system in place, perhaps just for certain segments of the company where a specified period each day is spent in insight mode.

One of the foundations of the WizeWell program is that it's flexible; each company has the freedom to develop a custom program that highlights the themes and Focus Phrases most important to the vision of that company.

For most companies, the optimum game plan will include moving once around the WizeWell Spiral in the first 6 weeks, and then tailoring the second round of the Spiral to specifically meet long-term goals. Our team will also work with yours to evolve a plan that adjusts in response to unexpected developments, and expands where needed in different regions of your employee base.

What About The 'Guidance" Part?

When saying "I am open to receive insight and guidance," an employee is opening not just to insight into the resolution of a problem, or the sudden realization of how to create a new product or service. There's something more to be tapped here as well:

As we mentioned in the beginning, each person on your team carries within their core of being a deeper voice of wisdom, which is closely linked to the creative process in that it taps directly into the whole-brain integrative function of the mind.

Let's look at the full Wikipedia definition of wisdom again, to see just how important this function of the mind really is, and how it integrates into the needs of business:

A) Wisdom is a deep understanding and realization that results in the ability to choose, or act, or inspire, in order to produce the optimum results with a minimum of time, energy, or thought.

B) Wisdom is the ability to effectively and efficiently apply perceptions and knowledge in order to produce desired results.

C) Wisdom is the comprehension of what is true or right, coupled with optimum judgment leading to right action.

D) A synonym for wisdom is insight.

Usually people think of wisdom as something that a few exceptional elderly people magically become filled with and impart to others. In fact, wisdom is an expanded whole-brain quality of integrated consciousness that anyone, or even a group together, can access at any time.

Furthermore wisdom is not some vague esoteric level of understanding and knowing – it's 'the ability to effectively and efficiently apply perceptions and knowledge in order to produce desired results'. This is the perfect definition of what every company in the world wants from each and every employee.

What we logically end up with here is the realization that taking time for and spending company money on manifesting short daily breaks during which employees at all levels pause and tune into their creative voice of insight and wisdom – this is good business, to say the least.

Creativity Cannot Be Forced

Perhaps one of the main reasons that there have not been concise programs like the WizeWell Process before in business is because <u>insight and wisdom cannot be manipulated</u>, they are functions of the mind that refuse to jump through managerial hoops.

The only way to encourage the innovative muse to come out of the cave of creation and bring blessings to a company is to stop all manipulation, quiet that chronic stressed-out pushy 'I'm gunna make this happen' function of the mind altogether on a regular basis – and passively and humbly open up to receive the effortless inflow of insight into the thinking mind.

Let's be honest – most of business is very masculine, aggressive, competitive, forceful. We're in broadcast mode most of the time at work, and traditionally our job definition has been to be constantly on the go, producing, pushing, manifesting with our ego muscle.

- The time has come to realize that this non-stop pushing at work does not always serve us best. It generates stress, it undermines our health, it generates fatigue and dissatisfaction and illness and confusion and all the rest.

We need to redefine work so that there's a built-in pulsation between being active and being receptive, between pushing and relaxing, between stressing and recharging – and between giving and receiving.

It's not just a curious biological coincidence that we have two entirely different functions of the mind. For clear survival-related reasons, we need both extremes in order to get through a hectic business day – there needs to be balance!

Our entire discussion here is about refocusing attention regularly at work in order to regain a healthy balance on all levels. You will need to decide what that balance will be in your particular company, but hopefully you see the logic and wisdom in purposefully acting to bring more balance into your workforce on the six key levels we're addressing here: physical, emotional, creative, productive, interactive, integrative.

Predictably Wise Leadership

In all organizations, no one wants to follow a leader who is not in touch with his or her inner voice of wisdom, that goes without saying. And yet it needs saying – because somehow we've mostly lost that clear understanding of what a leader truly is, or should be.

Look again at the first part of the wisdom definition:

> *Wisdom is a deep understanding and realization that results in the ability to choose, or act, or inspire, in order to produce the optimum results with a minimum of time, energy, or thought.*

For a leader to lead wisely, first there must come *'a deep understanding and realization'* – and this clarity comes to a leader who regularly takes time to quiet the high buzz of detail-fixation thinking, and enter into the whole-brain visionary function of the mind where deep understanding and realization emerge and radiate into inspired thought.

Then as a direct result of this inspiration pause, comes wise action – the *'ability to choose, or act, or inspire, in order to produce the optimum results with a minimum of time, energy, or thought.'*

Notice especially the words 'with a minimum of time, energy, or thought.' Obviously the people who wrote this definition of wisdom were business-savvy.

- Wisdom does include the survival factors of getting something done in minimum time, with minimum energy expended, with minimum stress, and also with a minimum of deductive rationalization.

How's that for a new definition of what a true leader is?

True leaders are those executives, teachers, public servants and visionaries who periodically pause to tune into their deeper whole-brain function ... so that they can perceive the whole of a situation, sense the natural and right organic flow, and then move confidently into action to manifest the deeper true vision.

We hope that the WizeWell Process can be of service to all leaders who want to stay tapped into that vital quality of consciousness that lets them know they are doing the right thing. We also acknowledge that leaders are a special breed that needs custom programs for implementing such a procedure into their stuffed agenda.

In this light, to end this chapter let's reflect upon this particular section of the wisdom definition:

Wisdom is the comprehension of what is true or right,
coupled with optimum judgment,
leading to right action.

Related to this process of comprehending right or wrong in a given situation, we all know deep-down that the brain is capable of tapping a higher wisdom that can directly sense and know right from wrong:

> **When we tap 'knowing' at this level**
> **and couple this with optimum judgment**
> **we can then move into right action.**

Item 5: Guaranteeing Employee Satisfaction

Click Here to Watch Item 5 Video

That's a very big word – guaranteed. Is it the duty of an employer to guarantee such a lofty thing as employee satisfaction? Furthermore what does 'satisfaction' really mean?

Satisfaction is that positive inner feeling in the heart and mind that makes employees want to continue working at your company – because they enjoy the work and the people, the atmosphere and the higher purpose of your company.

Very well documented studies show that satisfied employees work harder, they are more motivated, more creative, more empathic and more healthy than employees who are grumbling in their beards and complaining behind your back.

- Conversely, in our science-documentation section you'll find loads of research proving that unhappy dissatisfied employees make more errors, are sick or otherwise gone from work much more often, deliver considerably lower production, are less engaged, enter into conflict more often, and generate far fewer innovative ideas than employees who feel content at work.

So, logically – perhaps it's not the duty of an employer to guarantee satisfaction in the workplace, but based on long-term studies of productivity, wellness, engagement, communication and innovation, it's downright dangerous not to.

Consider the all-important quit rate of your company. Especially related to loss of key personnel, it's one of the main indicators of a healthy or floundering company. Boost employee satisfaction and you reduce your quit rate – and in so doing you create a more valuable company.

Employee satisfaction isn't just about wages and training programs and perks. Satisfaction is all about attitudes, emotions, and present-moment experience – so this is where we must focus in order to develop strategies that will positively impact your quit rate and all the other satisfaction-variables.

Satisfaction Is An Emotion

Realistically, how can a company boost employee satisfaction? Of necessity we must return here to the principles and research of cognitive science – and here's the key finding:

- Back in the 1960's at the University of Pennsylvania, the primary founder of cognitive therapy, Aaron Beck, demonstrated that most emotions emerge as whole-body responses (or reactions) to our habitual thoughts.

So … if you want someone to feel more satisfied at work, you will need to focus on inserting and reinforcing positive thoughts and healthy attitudes. And this must be done openly with zero manipulation.

Professor Beck demonstrated scientifically what wise folk had always noted – that very human being gets imprinted with the core one-liner attitudes of her or his parents during early childhood. That's just how life is – we learn not only how to talk, but also how to think and feel, from our parents during our first few years of life.

- This means that, like it or not, employees who join your company come pre-programmed with whatever attitudes they inherited from their parents and early social influences, hopefully somewhat modified by adult experience.

Probably your hiring practices are at least partly geared to bring people into your organization with attitudes that support rather than fight the atmosphere and vision of your company. But perhaps you don't have a specific system for evaluating the core attitudinal structure of potential employees.

The 30 Focus Phases of our program are clear indicators of whether a potential employee will be a bright light or a chronic downer to your company atmosphere. If applicants react negatively to more than three or four of the Focus Phrases, this is a red light to evaluate seriously.

- And yes, your company does have the right, and also the responsibility, to choose employees whose attitudes resonate with your company's vision.

If you make sure that new employees enter your company already affirming the 30 core themes of the WizeWell program or a similar system, and also have them continue to focus and reflect regularly upon these themes, you can be confident that you're actively optimizing worker satisfaction and performance.

Satisfaction … Guaranteed?

People in any group or tribe, family or team do have certain basic experiences and objectives that they hunger to receive:

- They need to feel secure and safe and protected.

- They need to know that if they do a good job, they'll be respected and rewarded accordingly.

- They need to experience regular exchanges of compassion, and an underlying sense of belonging.

- They need to feel passion for their work, and a sense of participating on a team that's doing good in the world.

- They need to feel free to enjoy themselves as they explore new ideas and ways of approaching their work.

- They need to feel that their employer genuinely cares for them and is nurturing not just their work value but their deeper potential and fulfillment.

These are not unreasonable needs – and if they're purposefully met, a company's quit rate will be quite low. To further this goal, the WizeWell program focuses adequate attention on these key satisfaction-variables so that employees feel their core needs are being honored and advanced.

Most companies already have a set of core values in place that at least theoretically express the vision of the company. What we're doing here is turning a set of theoretical statements into a living process that's ongoing, continually reinforcing the higher intent of your company.

The Practice Of Non-Manipulation

Let's now openly address the issue of mind management versus mind control. Employees will react vehemently, and rightly so, if they feel that their company is trying in any way to manipulate their attitudes and feelings at work. Not only does a company have zero right to try to manipulate the minds of its employees – such manipulation in the long run doesn't work.

In just the opposite direction, employees need to feel that their employer is actively allowing them to be who they really are. They also need to feel that they are being encouraged to grow and evolve and learn how to manifest their highest purpose and attainment.

- Most of the time during a workday, employees dutifully hold their focus of attention exactly where their employer needs them to, in order to further the work and success of the company. This is right and good, and nobody should complain – that's what work is all about.

However, we're suggesting that short paid breaks during the workday routine need to be inserted, where everyone focuses attention toward their shared vision of what it means to be a harmonious fulfilled person at work.

All 30 of the Focus Phrases aim attention in directions that:

- allow employees to feel good

- expand awareness rather than contract it

- nurture wellness rather than reduce it

- provide room for new experience and intuitive insight

- set the person free both emotionally and mentally

- wake up universal aspirations of creative expression

Allowing employees to regularly focus in these directions is just the opposite of manipulation – the process is a freeing experience. The only mind-management aspect is the required discipline needed in order to pause for a few minutes and focus attention in a particular previously-agreed-to direction.

Who's Having Fun Here?

Think for a moment of the ten brightest up-surging companies of the last 20 years: along with all the work, was it also just plain fun to work in these companies? Was there pure pleasure in being part of the Apple team? Sure there was, and why?

Companies like Apple somehow spontaneously tapped into and sustained that inner sense of joyful participation in a meaningful greater whole that we're now aiming to nurture purposefully.

Like creativity, enjoyment is a quality of consciousness that cannot be manipulated into existence – fun is fun because it's spontaneous, it's a gift, it flows unexpectedly into one's life experience all on its own. Try as it may, the ego cannot force joy to emerge; nor can a company dictate that everyone must enjoy their work experience.

All we can do is choose to actively focus company attention in the general direction of joy and contentment and fulfillment and creativity and all the other positive qualities of consciousness that we want at work … and regularly allow our employees to be open to receive.

This is the freedom and shared intent that your company can offer to your team, to show that you genuinely want to nurture employee satisfaction. And all you need to do is:

- Provide a company philosophy and vision that supports genuine enjoyment at work;

- Provide regular time and space for Breather Breaks;

- Provide helpful non-manipulative guidance as needed;

- Then ... get out of the way and allow the natural joyful unfolding to happen as it spontaneously will.

A key word here is 'spontaneous'. Usually work is defined as the opposite of spontaneous – it's supposed to be ordered and predictable and regimented and so forth and so on. Traditionally people were punished at work if they 'got out of line' and behaved outside established norms.

But the definition of work is evolving rapidly in the direction of allowing employees to:

- feel free to have sudden flashes of insights that generate joy and innovation

- feel free to smile and laugh – and enjoy the present moment even while getting one's work done

- feel free to behave spontaneously so that a sense of newness and discovery and play enters the workplace

Yes, discipline and routine and order are required at work. But, once again, there must be a balance between extremes. There must be time to let go and relax and just 'be' on a regular basis, if employees are to feel satisfied and content and downright happy on the job.

Setting The Breath Free – The Satisfaction Key

Let's take a deeper look at the foundation act of each Breather Break, in which the employee is given total freedom, and steady guidance, to temporarily stop doing anything at all at work, and instead to just 'be' ... to feel free and at peace and in harmony.

How we breathe is who we are. Physiologically there is no separation between how we think and feel, and how we're breathing.

- Each emotion that a person is feeling at any given moment will be expressed as a particular breathing pattern. Someone who is relaxed and confident will breathe more deeply, smoothly, and fully (not to mention more enjoyably) than someone caught up in worries, anger, boredom, sadness or grief.

Therefore, if you encourage your employees to regularly free up and expand their breathing depth and rhythm, their emotional and cognitive experience will directly improve as a result.

Because breathing can be consciously altered, we do have the power to positively influence our breathing, and thus to influence our emotional mood.

But again – moving in the direction of more control and manipulation is usually a bad call for the person's overall health and enjoyment. There are certainly extreme moments when emotions need to be controlled, and in the WizeWell program we teach 'emotional first aid' breath-control techniques that can work wonders.

In general, however, it's important to focus on helping employees set their breathing free, rather than further controlling it.

Stress disturbs the body's natural mechanisms for maintaining balance on all fronts – and this is nowhere more noticeable than in the breathing. As stressed thoughts, imaginations and emotions make the breathing shallow, irregular, and uptight, the whole organism suffers – sometimes drastically.

The body knows how to gain and maintain perfect bio-chemical balance. Focusing attention to the breath experience almost instantly generates a positive inner-directed change in the breathing – which in turn generates proper oxygen/CO_2 homeostasis. (see research in back that substantiates all this)

"I set my breathing free."

Say it … do it.

Inserting Wisdom and Vision

Based on traditional notions of work, it might seem that letting employees pause regularly for a Breather Break (where they tune in to reinvigorating feelings such as inner peace, relaxation, contentment, and joy) would be counter productive because they might shift permanently out of serious work gear.

Just the opposite actually happens. A properly-structured Breather Break grants employees a few highly-valued minutes during which they can catch their breath, regain their senses and recover their present-moment vitality … and then the break is over and they return to their work feeling refreshed, renewed, and ready to relate and perform at higher levels – while also continuing to enjoy themselves.

- Short periodic breaks from stress are like pausing for a few breaths while hiking up a mountain trail – a short breather break is rejuvenating, but it's important not to pause too long or you lose your momentum.

Breather Breaks will positively impact breathing, and that's important for reducing stress. But equally important during these short breaks is the insertion of a particular cognitive statement, as we've seen, that aims attention directly toward one of the 30 primary life themes.

As we'll see in Part Two, each Focus Phrase of the WizeWell Process is driven by a universal psychological

and philosophical need and realization. We all know deep-down these primal truths of what makes a fulfilling life – but we tend to never focus in these crucial directions, and our personal and business lives suffer on all fronts as a result.

Each Focus Phrase is designed to stimulate an inner response that is uplifting and invigorating, liberating and transformative. In Part Two we'll examine each of these 30 WizeWell insertions in depth, so that you can evaluate the intended impact of each day's Breather Break theme, and also discover the underlying logic of the order of presentation and employment.

Boosting Charisma and Sales

Why does the basic act of shifting one's attention out of lost-in-thought mode to present-moment sensory alertness induce important improvements in mental performance, stress levels, and so forth?

Linear deductive thinking is a two-dimensional happening in the brain – thought is a flat line without depth. As soon as the mind shifts away from thought into sensation (air flowing through the nose) and then expands to experience several sensations at once, the mind instantly expands into a full three-dimensional experience. All of a sudden there's volume and space; the body comes alive in the here and now; the person feels more vibrant, energized, fully 'here'.

- From a business-performance perspective this shift has remarkable power because business actually takes place in the three-dimensional here and now, not in the past or the future.

Learning to shift rapidly from 'lost in thought' into present-moment experiencing is a primary tool for making sure that

employees relating with customers and any other face-to-face or phone encounter are genuinely present, and thus able to have a positive impact.

All successful communication requires this in-the-body presence and quality of heart-to-heart empathy. We all spend a lot of time lost in our own thinking minds, and this is an important part of our at-work contribution. But we also need to be able to regularly 'return to our senses' as fast and smoothly as possible, when it's time for another encounter at work.

Are These Positive Affirmations?

Positive affirmations are often nothing more than wishful thinking, ungrounded in realistic personal experience, and fixated on hopeful future developments that might be entirely unrealistic.

The WizeWell Focus Phrases don't play fantasy games at all – instead they aim attention solidly in practical inner directions that everyone wants to move in. They focus attention not toward some fanciful possible future imagination, but toward a present-moment experience.

At deeper levels, the purpose of a Focus Phrase is to aim attention toward the optimum condition possible for human achievement. Most people are far from the total fulfillment of a Focus Phrase, but everyone has the distinct potential of step by step naturally moving in this direction.

Focus Phrases are based on the fact that energy flows where attention goes …we advance in the directions we focus attention toward – it's that simple, and that profound.

For instance, consider Focus Phrase #8:

"I honor and love myself, just as I am."

We all know that self-judgment is deadly, and that we need to love ourselves unconditionally if we're to blossom and flower into our higher potential. But still, most people go around hitting themselves over the head because of old one-liner negative programmings and self-judgments.

So what's to be done? A large body of research in cognitive therapy has demonstrated that bringing a positive Focus Phrase regularly to mind that states a realistic hopeful intent, such as honoring and loving ourselves just as we are, will step by step generate a natural movement in that desired direction. That's the underlying strategy of Focus Phrases – and as extensive research documents, it works very well.

- Look at it this way, as cognitive science outlines: If you want to go to Philadelphia, you're never going to get there (except by random chance) if you don't bring the thought to mind, "I want to go to Philadelphia." Conversely, if you do regularly bring this thought to mind and hold it there, you'll naturally elicit the logical response of going into action to see about getting a train ticket or finding some other means of acting on your intent.

A successful Focus Phrase will be a carefully-designed statement of intent that stimulates immediate inner movement toward that intent: Say it – do it. However, if you just read it once rather than say it often to yourself to imbed it in your mind, you'll probably forget the intent … and not achieve your inner goal. Thus the need for a daily reinforcement/reminder program.

These particular 30 Focus Phrases satisfy most employee's psychological needs and intentions because they have been carefully developed and are based on an in-depth overview of human-potential psychology.

- We spent over ten years identifying the universal causes of human emotional suffering, and also studied the shared human strivings and deeper desires that transcend particular cultural differences. We then condensed these universal psychological needs into our 30 intent statements.

Although some of the Focus Phrases will at first seem unrelated to business success, rest assured that each and every one is necessary from the perspective of cognitive science, in order to assure that employees are emotionally and mentally balanced, refreshed, and inspired.

Part TWO:

A Unified Wellness/Productivity Plan

Click Here to Watch Part 2 Video

In both science and philosophy, there's always an ongoing quest to discover the shortest, most effective and universal perspective on any given situation.

Related to the current stress-versus-health theme, great stacks of academic research and a numerous theories and techniques have come forth with claims that they've found important answers to key parts of the stress crisis – but still there are very few game plans that deal cohesively and effectively with the causal agents of stress at work.

- Running on both perspiration and inspiration, our team has now finalized an integrated and hopefully very-potent understanding of the overall situation.

We have identified 6 core themes and 30 essential Focus Phrases that, taken as a whole, do fully address the stress crisis – and when presented properly over time, deliver predictable long-term relief that positively impacts all aspects of a company's wellbeing.

From an at-work perspective, it's now clear that stress negatively impacts employee wellbeing on the following six levels: 1) physical, 2) emotional, 3) creative, 4) productive, 5) interactive, and 6) integrative. Each level must be effectively dealt with, in order to transcend the mental and emotional pressures that otherwise undermine the health and performance of your team.

To gain a solid overview of the WizeWell Process, let's review these 6 themes in turn, and discuss the 24 active Focus Phrases and their specific impact on these themes. (We'll discuss the additional 6 Review Phrases at the end of this section.)

First: What Exactly Is A Focus Phrase?

Focus Phrases are present-moment experience-based mental choices, based on cognitive science, that aim one's attention in important life directions on a regular basis.

What we focus upon regularly is what we manifest ... so let's take charge of where we focus our attention, in order to stimulate positive growth, success, and wellness.

Theme 1: "Physical Wellbeing"
reducing stress – boosting inner presence

Each morning, your employees arrive as physical beings packing whatever charge of positive or negative tensions, emotions, and symptoms that they carry in general, or that have developed while they were off-work. As they come into the office, they broadcast either a positive or negative presence that in turn impacts both their quality of work, and their ability to relate successfully with their team and clients.

- In principle all employees, when engaged at work, are being paid to hold their focus of attention away from personal past-and-future memories, imaginations and plans, and to maintain full attentiveness toward the present work at hand. Too often, however, people are being continually distracted from work by unrelated past-future mental activity.

The wisest move when an employee arrives at work is to give them the opportunity to pause and take a few deep breaths, and shift their attention fully into the present moment – rather than remaining stuck in personal memories and worries, or vaguely day-dreaming of their possible future.

- It's to everyone's advantage to encourage employees to also shift naturally and regularly into a brighter attitude toward the day in general – this shift will deliver tangible rewards equally to employees and employers.

This first week of Focus Phrases regularly exercises the primary attention muscle that returns an employee's focus to active engagement in present-moment work.

The very first Focus Phrase carries special power with every word, stating the universal human desire to simply feel good:

- "I choose to enjoy this moment."

~~~~~~~~~~~~~~~~~~~~~~~~

The following three Focus Phrases continue this movement into present-moment presence and enjoyment by focusing attention exactly toward the primal sensations that keep us alive and healthy – the breath experience. As noted before, great health/performance benefits are engendered by helping employees to more regularly return their focus to what is called mindfulness

– where one's physical presence in the present moment is made conscious.

If indeed most of our stress is being caused by chronic worried and stressed-out thought flows, surely the most rational move to ease that negative condition is to quiet the thoughts that are causing the condition, As mentioned earlier, this is best accomplished by shifting full attention toward the sensory breathing experience, and whole-body presence.

- This Breath Shift process is the foundation of all we do in this program, because regaining one's senses in the present moment is the essential first step in breaking free from stress and fatigue, and tapping higher clarity and creativity at work.

The full week-one flow of Focus Phrases that activate the rapid shift into conscious breathing are as follows:

"I choose to enjoy this moment."

"I feel the air flowing in and out of my nose."

"I also feel the movements in my chest and belly as I breathe."

"I'm aware of my whole body, here in this present moment."

~~~~~~~~~~~~~~~~~~~~~~~~~

The very act of saying these focal statements generates the desired response of waking up to the here and now where all business actually takes place. And, as soon as one's awareness is focused on the breath experience, a person's breathing begins to expand and change for the better, to relax and deepen.

- Something of high benefit happens ... tense thoughts become quiet and stress is almost immediately relieved.

NOTE: If a person simply tries to focus on their breath experience without using Focus Phrases (as in traditional mindfulness meditation) a similar result is often attained – but it takes 20-30 minutes to attain. By employing new cognitive tools like our Focus Phrases, 20-30 minutes can be condensed into 1-2 minutes, once an employee gets good at the shifting process.

Practice does make perfect in this regard – therefore, each day of the 6-week WizeWell Process, all four of the short video inserts begin with purposefully exercising this basic mental shift into full whole-body conscious-breath presence.

- The first 6-week cycle of the WizeWell Spiral guides your employees through the 'return to your senses' mindfulness procedure a total of 120 times. Quite soon, for most employees, this alert state becomes second nature – it's one of the most valuable at-work tools ever devised for low-stress high-performance action.

Theme 2: "Emotional Wellbeing"
regaining inner balance and harmony

This second week of the WizeWell Process builds on the first week's essential here-and-now platform by addressing the four primary causes of emotional stress and discomfort that employees often bring to the workplace.

- Emotions usually arise as bodily feelings provoked by thoughts that we're chronically holding in the back of our minds. These bodily reactions (hormonal secretions provoking all manner of imbalance in the system) then wreak havoc with mental performance and wellness.

Old mental attitudes, prejudices, outmoded beliefs and fear-based apprehensions are notorious for sticking their hoary heads right in the middle of an otherwise-satisfactory workday, provoking emotional reactions that turn into bodily tension – that's what psychological stress is all about.

Fighting fire with fire, in Week 2 we introduce 4 Focus Phrases that can work wonders in defusing the root source of emotional symptoms such as confusion, anxiety, fatigue, and impatience. By holding these Focus Phrases in mind, worries and judgments fall away, emotional honesty and empathy rises, self-esteem is boosted, and related benefits ensue.

~~~~~~~~~~~~~~~~~~~~~~~

Once an employee is attuned to his or her breathing and physical presence, it's essential to acknowledge whatever stress-related emotions are currently gripping one's body. As employees continues to stay aware of their breath experience, we introduce the following Focus Phrase:

- "I'm ready to experience all of the feelings in my throat, my heart, and belly."

Therapists have known for decades that the first step in transcending negative emotions is to pause and simply feel their presence in one's body. It's amazing how often people go through their whole day without consciously tuning into their own feelings – especially the negative ones. This fifth Focus Phrase accomplishes this goal with gusto.

~~~~~~~~~~~~~~~~~~~~~~~

The next step is to use special Focus Phrases to focus on letting go of chronic fixations on the negative, and instead focusing on positive feelings. To initiate this process, we first deal with the primary negative emotion, fear by inserting this elicitor statement into the workday:

- "I let go of all my stress and worry, and feel peaceful inside."

As mentioned before, the motto of the WizeWell Process is "Say it – do it!" State your clear intent to shift from stress posture to its opposite (inner peace) and by the very act of proclaiming your intent, allow it to happen. Let go of the worries, and focus on inner calm and clarity – peace.

~~~~~~~~~~~~~~~~~~~~~~~~~~

Once this intent is stated, the next emotional honcho to deal directly with is the chronic mental act of judging the world and the workplace as not good enough, as somehow faulty. This results in one of the most deadly pair of of emotions – rejection and denial.

Employees who chronically hold judgmental thoughts about the world dominant in their minds, by definition separate themselves from full participation in the present moment – because they're fighting against it.

We gently counter this conditioned stance with the following all-encompassing Focus Phrase:

- "I accept the world just as it is, right now."

As soon as this thought is inserted into the workplace, employees go through a remarkable transformation – their very act of accepting the reality of their present moment enables them to perceive it clearly, and rather than being in denial, they are suddenly in participation with that workplace reality. This enables them to respond appropriately, and advance the company intent successfully.

Again, we're talking about process here, not miracles. But by holding this Focus Phrase in mind throughout an entire workday, people do naturally begin to shift their attitudinal stance from non-stop judgment, into tentative acceptance.

- This is important because nobody fights reality and wins. After all, the world is as it is right now. First we must accept a situation in order to perceive it realistically. Only then can we initiate actions that positively evolve that situation. In essence, this is the underlying dynamic of positive change in a company.

~~~~~~~~~~~~~~~~~~~~~~~

The final Focus Phrase for Week 2 is perhaps the deepest-hitting, because it shifts a person's attitude regarding themselves in less judgmental, more uplifting directions. Most people go around hitting themselves over the head with outmoded one-liner self-judgments that directly undermine their performance and success. Here's the Focus Phrase that most effectively, over time, defuses self-judgment and raises self-esteem:

- "I honor and love myself, just as I am."

Of course, when first encountering this Focus Phrase, most of your employees are not honoring and loving themselves just as they are. They've been programmed in their society to see themselves as highly flawed, as never entirely adequate – and so they chronically try to improve themselves, hoping that at some future date they'll arrive at that point where they're finally entirely okay.

- It's now a proven fact that employees with low self esteem perform poorly compared with employees with high self-esteem – so what can be done about this? Psychologically, because the ingrained negative one-liners are so deep in the psyche, all we can do is state the universal desire we all feel, and let this resonate in our minds for an entire day at work: "I honor and love myself just as I am ..."

By introducing this clearly-stated positive universal goal into one's mind four times during an entire day at work ... something happens. A seed is planted. And in the context of the following Focus Phrases, that seed will sprout and blossom.

Theme 3: "Creative Wellbeing"
unleashing the insight muse

At this point in the WizeWell Process your employees have entertained in their minds 8 potent Focus Phrases that help bring them into the present moment, tune them into their core feelings, and help them let go of old outworn reactions.

Furthermore, they have learned how to temporarily quiet the flow of disrupting thoughts through their minds, so that they experience for at least a few moments a few times a day, an inner quality of consciousness that's peaceful, quiet, receptive, and reality-attuned.

It's time to insert a Focus Phrase that truly blows the dullness of the conditioned mind. In the spirit of awakening sudden flashes of insight that stimulate innovative vision ... that in turn leads to those creative ideas that make your company truly great ... here's a Focus Phrase worth its proverbial weight in gold:

- "I am open to receive ... insight and guidance."

As we discussed in Part One, most employees most of the time are simply not in the right frame of mind to receive those invaluable flashes of insight that result in breakthrough thinking.

What would happen in your company if you paid your employees 4 times a day to take just a couple of minutes to quiet their over-busy minds, tune into their higher creative muse ... and open up to flashes of insight concerning all

your various company issues currently begging improvement and breakthrough?

- Give employees a Breather Break 4 times a day. Help them shift from chronic point-fixation to seeing the whole at once. Let them temporarily expand their awareness so that they're open to receive exactly what your company vision craves – those sudden integrative whole-brain realizations that bring new vision and creation into the pulse of your company's everyday life.

~~~~~~~~~~~~~~~~~~~~~~~~~~

That done, what could follow? Well, how about the final 'cognitive tune-in' step that makes sure all your employees are resonant with, rather than out of joint with, the underlying creative power and glory of this entire universe.

- "I feel connected with my creative source."

Beyond any particular philosophical belief system, our human community has now come to accept the scientific fact that this universe was created by some radical transcendent force and intelligence and presence ... that our individual ego selves either habitually fight against, or surrender and experience the empowering feeling of being unified with.

After all, who wants a leader, or an employee, who doesn't feel connected with their creative source? And really – what company thrives that's chronically disconnected from this creative source?

This that this is not really such a lofty idea. It is not in fact a thought at all – it's a sensory whole-body feeling. "I feel connected ..."

- Our experience has shown that most companies, upon deeper reflection, know that they survive and thrive based ultimately on whether or not the majority of their workforce and leadership is in practice regularly connecting at the feeling level with their shared creative source.

We're therefore of necessity insistent on going all the way logically to the very epicenter of productivity and harmony on your team – connectivity with your creative source.

~~~~~~~~~~~~~~~~~~~~~~~

At this point in the WizeWell Process it's prime time to reflect on the parallel question of purpose – why does each employee on your team get up in the morning and come to work? When all is said and done, why are we here, really?

We've found a clear universal answer, a four-tier response that, when held in mind throughout the work day, can transform every moment of that day:

> "I am here to serve ... to love
> ... to prosper ... and enjoy myself."

Because this 4-part statement seems so short and simple, some people try to find a fifth or sixth core purpose that motivates human beings around the globe. But except for neurotic or psychotic distortions of these reasons for going into action each new day, these four root purposes seem to cover all bases for most people.

- And note this: when an employee is disconnected from one of more of these four reasons for participating in the business world, that person will usually begin to malfunction and generate difficulties for his or her team.

Therefore we recommend not only devoting a full day each 6 weeks to all-company focus on this statement of purpose – we also encourage regular open discussions on how all 4 themes are required for a balanced, healthy, happy life.

~~~~~~~~~~~~~~~~~~~~~~~~~~

To end Week 3, we now introduce a Focus Phrase that's again very short and at the same time quite sublime. This week began with a focus on receiving insight – on being passive and quiet and open to listening to one's inner voice of wisdom. The week ends with a strong call to action, in order to manifest inflowing wisdom and insight at the highest levels possible:

- "I am ready to act with courage and integrity."

Yes, a meditative peaceful insightful state of mind is important to engender regularly, in order to reduce stress and boost creative wellbeing. But work remains work – therefore the ultimate outcome of the WizeWell Process must also include productive courageous action.

And what about the word 'integrity'? We've recently witnessed far too much greed, dishonesty, cowardice and out-and-out criminal acts in the financial world. For a time it actually looked as if being disingenuous was the trick to success in the business world. However, in the long run we all know in our hearts that a positive sense of right and wrong, of high values and sincere behavior, affords the greatest sense of joy, success, and fulfillment in life.

Therefore one of the prime intentions that all wise leaders want to feel resonating throughout their workforce from CEO on down is this twelfth Focus Phrase: "I am ready to act with courage and integrity."

Theme 4: "Productive Wellbeing"
augmenting manifestation power

It's wonderful for employees to be granted time during the workday to recover their inner sense of wellbeing and enjoyment even while on the job. But the parallel reality is that work is still work, and employees are being paid to help the company not only survive, but thrive.

- Human beings in general also like to feel that they're needed, that they're creative and innovative and pack the power to manifest their dreams, and help fulfill the vision of their company.

In other words, in Week 4 it's time to shift to using Focus Phrase technology to directly stimulate higher productivity in the workplace, and devote attention to regularly empowering your company's vision mandate. We do this through unifying an employee's personal vision with the vision of their company.

Each employee carries his or her core needs and desires that reflect a creative vision of what the good life consists of. In harmonious healthy situations, their individual vision and the vision of their company should be highly congruent.

- Why this congruency? Because the long-term wellbeing of one's company is what sustains much of a person's personal vision, because the financial success of their company directly supports their personal wellbeing.

In this light, the four Focus Phrases of Week 4 guide employees into making contact with their deeper needs, and holding their creative vision of the good life firmly in mind – so that the flow of manifestation power into the workplace is optimized.

We begin Monday of Week 4 with a strong clear reinforcement of the calm quiet-mind quality of consciousness that enables employees to tap fully into their creative potential at work:

- "My mind is quiet ... I am here in this moment."

As employees continue through the day, this Focus Phrase will create a special atmosphere in the workplace where everyone is alert, responsive, and perceptive to the new – with a minimum of old ideas and projections that interfere with 'seeing the new'. In other words, everyone is in optimum mental mode for performing well and receiving flashes of innovative thinking.

~~~~~~~~~~~~~~~~~~~~~~~~~

What drives a company to high success is always the passion of its employees for the higher vision of the company. Human beings are motivated by their own inner needs and desires – and when individual needs and company needs are congruent, manifestation power rises up in the center of that company.

So the next step in our process of tapping manifestation power at work is to help employees tune strongly into their inner passions and desires, using this seminal Focus Phrase:

- "I feel connected with my deeper needs."

One of the recent innovations in psychological research has been the clarification of where the power to create actually emerges from in the human organism. Great ideas on their own don't actually accomplish anything. They require the injection of passion into the equation, for action to come into being and concrete manifestation of a vision to happen.

Thus the necessity of this Focus Phrase that turns employee attention directly toward the true powerhouse of company vision – their own passion for that vision.

We now come to another psychological insight – the logical observation that for a vision to step by step move from idea to physical expression, that vision must already at some level be perfect and complete in the visionary realms of one's mind.

Throughout the WizeWell Process we're training employees to pause and tap their whole-brain integrative mental function where they access the power to create a perfect fulfilled vision which then guides them into manifesting that vision.

That's what company vision is all about – everyone holding their ideal goal in mind, and unleashing their passion for creating this ideal goal as a physical manifestation.

So the next Focus Phrase, even though at first it might seem a bit esoteric, is actually the nuts and bolts needed to manifest the higher intent of your company:

- "My creative vision is right now perfect and complete."

Something truly explosive happens in the workplace when employees spend a whole day together holding this potent Focus Phrase in their minds ... step by step these words penetrate to intuitive/integrative levels of consciousness, and reinforce the union of passion and creativity.

~~~~~~~~~~~~~~~~~~~~~~~~

Now we're ready for the pay-off of this week, with a seemingly-simple statement aiming attention exactly and continuously toward the point of creation at work:

- "Each new moment is manifesting my vision."

We started this fourth week by returning the employee's focus of attention to the present moment, because this is where all innovative action takes place. When employees aren't focused in the here-and-now, they simply aren't in position to bring anything creative into being at work.

When people begin to consciously realize that 'right here right now' is where they're manifesting their dream, suddenly each moment at work becomes electric with creative energy. That's the optimum state that you want your employees to remain in, so that company vision becomes continually expressed by everyone.

Almost surely during this 4th week of the WizeWell Process you'll want to initiate discussions concerning your particular company vision, so that these 4 Focus Phrases become fully immersed in the particular higher vision you're leading your company toward.

Theme 5: "Interactive Wellbeing"
nurturing present-moment trust and mutual acceptance

A company is a team of human beings working together for the higher good, and also interacting with people outside the company in order to cooperate in the planetary economic organism that sustains us all. Therefore it's vital to spend a full week now helping your employees to relate with optimum heart-felt harmony and creative communication.

Most people most of the time are stuck in non-stop broadcast mode – they're thinking and talking. But successful communication requires each person to regularly shift entirely out of broadcast mode, into receive mode.

- We found this true earlier, related to receiving flashes of insight and tapping creative power. It's equally important for receiving information and insights from other people. That's what communication is all about.

Everyone knows of and wants to tap the power of being a truly good listener. Focus Phrases can help aim our intent exactly in this direction – so let's strike fire and state our intent with no hemming and hawing – just say it ... and begin to do it:

- "I am a good listener."

As we'll explain to your employees in this Monday's video training, listening doesn't just mean you stop talking and let someone else talk – it means that you also quiet your mind temporarily, and turn off that robotic cognitive function that's continually thinking of what you're going to say in response.

Listening means being truly receptive – trusting the other person's input, and allowing it to resonate within you. Then the other person feels that 'they've been heard' – and genuine communication and team spirit come into being.

- This is especially important in service and sales relating. Throughout this program we're teaching your employees how to temporarily quiet their mind, focus on their breathing and whole-body presence – so that they can be truly present and responsive to clients and customers.

~~~~~~~~~~~~~~~~~~~~~~~~~

The next Focus Phrase of this week deals with the universal human tendency to be in judgment mode most of the time. Nobody likes to feel judged, and yet we go around judging everybody else habitually. This is yet another old defensive programming that doesn't serve us – and we can actively shift our focus in the opposite direction by choosing to hold the following Focus Phrase in the back of our mind throughout the day:

- "I accept everyone I work with, just as they are."

Most of the world's religions (at least in theory) consider mutual acceptance and unconditional love as primary pillars of their spiritual vision. And you'll find that heart-felt brightness very often floods into your company when employees hold this statement of intent primary for a whole day. Furthermore, as with all the Focus Phrases of this program, this positive impact will continue to resonate in your workplace far the future.

Employees learn long-term lessons from the unique experience engendered by each Focus Phrase. That's the intent of this program as a whole ... to permanently imbue your workplace with this set of 30 core statements that represent and amplify the higher vision of your company.

~~~~~~~~~~~~~~~~~~~~~~

The third Focus Phrase of Week 5 is equally important for team relating, because it reinforces a human quality that lies at the heart of all valuable communication in your company. All too often, employees are afraid to really speak their minds, to trust their own sparks of insight, and share them vocally – and your company suffers from this inhibition.

What can be done to reverse this inhibitory tendency? Again, the shortest and most decisive Focus Phrase will prove the most evocative:

- "I trust my spontaneous thoughts and expressions."

Creativity and innovation come into being at work only when spontaneity is not only allowed, but openly encouraged.

- So it makes solid business sense to set your employees free as often as possible, within this context of creating space for new ideas to come flowing into your company. This Focus Phrase especially needs to be imbedded on the wall loud and clear.

A company is a team – team spirit rules the day. And each member of your team needs to regularly experience three core qualities of togetherness, that act as the cement of a successful unified organization. Here they are in a concise statement of intent:

- "I feel safe, confident, and valued on my team."

As with all the Focus Phrases, this is an expression of a person's deeper vision expressing the direction they want to move in. Predictably, where attention goes … energy flows.

Safety, confidence and, personal worth are all subjective perceived conditions. There are of course times when realistically a person is neither safe nor valued on a team – and it's time to move on to another team

But all too often, old negative attitudes impinge on the present situation and pollute the team atmosphere. This Focus Phrase is designed to step by step override habitual self-judgment and anxiety, by aiming attention toward the positive option that most people can feel in their company.

- This Focus Phrase, like many of the others, naturally encourages discussion on a team, so that everyone has the chance to air their uncertainties, become more realistic in their feelings related to the group, and grow emotionally.

We do step by step manifest our dominant vision in the world. If it's negative, we end up living in a living hell. If it's positive, we move steadily in that direction - we begin to feel safer, more confident, and more valued on our team …

~~~~~~~~~~~~~~~~~~~~~~~~

Theme 6: "Integrative Wellbeing"
maximizing long-term health and fulfillment

We had originally hoped to have just 12 Focus Phrases for this program – but as you can see, each and every statement of intent that we've covered thus far is important for a company's overall wellbeing and success. And there are four final Focus Phrases that must also be included here – in fact they are among the most important.

Perhaps the greatest breakthrough in defining work has been the paradigm shift from perceiving employees as bio-robots performing a set of physical or mental tasks, to seeing them as unique integrated whole-body individuals who are conscious participants in the moment-to-moment unfolding of your company's higher vision.

The WizeWell Process is one expression of this rapid shift toward tapping the full integrated potential of each individual on your team. Employees are assets of the highest value – but only when they're set free to discover and express their authentic personal vision of what's happening in the workplace. In this spirit, here's one of the most powerful Focus Phrases imaginable:

- "I feel in touch with my authentic presence."

Of course, some of your employees when first encountering this statement won't even know what's meant by authentic presence, because indeed, they don't feel in touch with this foundation quality of their personality. But the magic of saying and holding in mind a Focus Phrase for an entire day is that it begins to permeate and resonate and wake up new insights ...

... and by the end of the day, each employee will most certainly feel at least somewhat more in touch with their authentic presence. Once these verbal seeds are planted in the mind, they do continue to grow and flower into conscious expression.

~~~~~~~~~~~~~~~~~~~~~~~~

We move now to yet another Focus Phrase that strikes to the heart of what it means to be innovative and happy at work. All your employees were once young children filled with the natural urge and ability to play creatively, expressing their integrated capacity all day long when allowed to.

What would happen in your company if you openly gave all your employees permission to bring their inner child to work each morning, to participate in the creative evolution of your company?

- Is this risky? Maybe some of your employees might be too playful, have too much fun at work. But the risk will prove well worth the effort – because when the inner child of your employees is not allowed in the workplace, that workplace is very dull and uncreative.

The next Focus Phrase that unleashes the passionate free spirit that's ultimately responsible for so much business success:

- "My inner child is free to play creatively at work."

The theme of week 6, integrative wellbeing, means that each of your employees is bringing both their creative inner child to work, and also their responsible adult personality. It's the integration of the two that we're encouraging, the youthful spirit of free play integrated into all the more-adult dimensions of the workplace.

~~~~~~~~~~~~~~~~~~~~~~~~

Fatigue is one of the most disastrous end-results of chronic stress. Medical research shows how stress provokes the secretion of a whole host of action-geared hormones into the bloodstream, which in turn burn up energy reserves and leave employees feeling drained, dull, moody and 'half here' at work.

- Following months and even years of habitual stress, most employees develop unspoken one-liners related to their feeling that they don't have much energy, that they run out of juice easily, and can't quite muster the charge needed to perform at truly great levels of excellence.

In redefining work, something must be done at the energy level to reverse this ingrained attitude that there just isn't enough energy available to accomplish great things.

Once employees begin to reduce the root cause of at-work stress, as they're learning to in this program, they also need to actively let go of their negative one-liners about not having enough energy. As discussed earlier, cognitive science indicates the importance of defusing negative one-liners by inserting realistic positive one-liners into the mind on a regular basis.

What are the optimum words that will aim employees in the uplifting direction of realizing that they're once again beginning to have more physical and emotional energy?

- "I have deep reserves of energy and compassion."

Note that we include emotional energy here along with physical energy. There's nothing worse than relating with someone who feels drained emotionally and doesn't have any energy for heart-to-heart relating.

- As the stress goes down, and present-moment breath awareness becomes a positive habit, employees do begin to tap into reserves of energy that they forgot they even had ... and their fatigue patterns begin to shift into smooth-energy patterns that serve them beautifully in all contexts.

We now come to the final Focus Phrase, and return to where we began: redefining work so that employees get their job done, but don't go into stress to get that job done.

Working rapidly and effectively does not cause stress. In fact studies show that people thrive on doing a good job quickly and efficiently. Health and satisfaction problems arise, as we've seen, only when people are pushed beyond their natural ability to do a job well.

Employees must be honored as human beings whose integrity is never violated on any level – that's an essential foundation stone in our new definition of work. This means that employers have the right to expect fast and efficient work, but they don't have the right to pressure employees beyond healthy limits.

The win-win solution is to team up with your employees and step by step manifest a workplace where rushing and hurrying are seen for what they are – chronic stressors that undermine the health and success of everyone on your team, and lower the value of the company's stock in the process.

We've already reviewed scientific research showing how people begin to malfunction when hurried. Somehow, management must manage the at-work show so that undo chronic rushing and hurrying is minimized – and one of the best ways to accomplish this goal is to help each employee hold this Focus Phrase in mind all day long:

- "I work fast and efficiently – but I don't hurry."

Of course, sometimes it's necessary to push, but there's it doesn't make sense to push employees so fast and stressfully that the next day they take a sick leave and don't show up at all. Pacing is everything – and attitude determines pacing. This final Focus Phrase will predictably reduce stress, and also boost performance, creativity and satisfaction. Say it – do it.

Fridays: Summary Programs & Focus Phrases

Following four days of programming and Focus Phrases, each Friday we offer a special summary of the week where employees are guided through all four Focus Phrases – and then taught a Summary Focus Phrase for that week.

Below is a list of the Summary Focus Phrases which employees learn on Friday and take home with them for the weekend. Note that each represents a clear choice:

Week 1: "I choose to breathe freely, and feel good."

Week 2: "I choose to trust all of my feelings."

Week 3: "I choose to nurture inspiration and wisdom."

Week 4: "I choose to create what's really needed."

Week 5: "I choose to participate in trust, joy, and harmony."

Week 6: "I choose to feel calm, bright, healthy and whole."

For people with weekly schedules that don't match this standard schedule, employees will receive custom schedules to fit their workweek. Also, on Fridays we recommend that your team divide into pods of around 10 people per pod, and meet for 15-30 minutes for an informal discussion of their experiences with the Focus Phrases of that week. We will provide a set of discussion questions to stimulate conversation. This weekly sharing can be very helpful on many fronts.

~~~~~~~~~~~~~~~~~~~~~~~~

Part THREE:

In The Zone ... All The Time?

Click Here to Watch Part 3 Video

A Qualitatively New At-Work Modality

This is truly a remarkable period of history businesswise – we've reached the point where, finally, what is seen as good and best and required for a company's employees is also optimum operational practice for the employer and stockholders.

Thus we come to our redefinition of work as a mutually-beneficial non-combative relationship where reason, wisdom, compassion and cooperation are openly allowed to rule the day.

As you perhaps know, corporations came into being in 16th century Switzerland as what were then called Gemeinschafts – publically-created local organizations that truly had a life of their own because they were owned by the community and dedicated to performing public works that everyone in the community needed.

- What a wild ride corporations have had since those early days, swept along by the wild unpredictable tide of human needs, desires, vision and potential. Always, there have been both employees, leaders and owners participating in the corporate process. And always there have been consumers ready to exchange their money for corporate services and products.

And throughout, as we've seen in this discussion, the fundamental corporate asset that has enabled us all to prosper has been that quality called 'clarity of heart and mind' that enables co-workers to see a situation clearly, evaluate the situation calmly, apply experience and reason to the situation – and when necessary pause and tap into deeper reservoirs of creativity, compassion and wisdom that generate a superior game plan that leads us beyond the dilemma.

Our primary dilemma right now in the workplace is chronic stress and employee breakdown, manifesting as mental confusion, faulty thinking, physical and emotional fatigue, worker dissatisfaction, chronic illness, emotional conflict and a host of related at-work difficulties.

The solution to this dilemma can be clean and simple – we need to focus full company attention each day toward commonly-shared goals and values, and help each employee to consciously manage her or his own mind so that clarity and balance, vitality and cooperation are predictably and enjoyably sustained.

To do otherwise or do nothing at all would not be a wise act, considering the pressing reality of the current situation. The courageous act will be to trust human nature a bit more at work, and employ mental-focus systems that progressively set employees free to tap their deeper potential, and bring this potential into play regularly at work.

In The Zone More Often

Everyone knows that rare elated feeling of being totally in tune and on top of one's day – of feeling inspired and empowered, empathic and entertaining, relaxed and graceful … that feeling of being in the zone, even at work.

Breather Breaks and the 30 Focus Phrases that empower them have the clear directive of purposefully helping people shift into the zone at work – not just rarely, but more and more often. Why not aim to develop a company that's in the zone all the time?

Being in the zone doesn't have to mean that you're athletically in action or bubbling over with great ideas. Being in the zone at work means staying in touch with your whole-body presence, your breathing, and your higher aspirations, while you go about your everyday duties.

• Being in the zone means keeping your spirit burning bright, your mind expanded to include the intuitive modes of consciousness, and your heart connected with your deeper source of compassion and wisdom.

We would like to formally offer you the challenge of redefining your company as a team that aspires to be in the zone … all the time.

Now that the psychological technologies are in place at a reasonable cost of time and money, it's logical to assume that companies that actively nurture in the zone mindsets at work will out-perform those that ignore this higher goal of maximizing performance through maximizing employee focus and radiance.

• As mentioned several times here, the creation of a high-focus company is not accomplished with a short 'transformation' commitment. Employee focus and health need to not only be temporarily raised up, but constantly sustained. In this spirit, we've designed the WizeWell Process as a spiral engagement, not a start-to-finish project.

In the WizeWell Spiral, your company moves (hopefully all together) through the first 6-week process, and then spirals up through another round of the 6-week process. Each time your team moves through a full immersion in all 30 Focus Phrases, they go deeper and higher into awakening their buried potential and bringing more of themselves to work each morning!

Executive Programs

It's one thing to be a sailor on a ship caught in a threatening storm – it's a qualitatively-different experience to be the captain of that ship. In this regard, the WizeWell Process is not intended just for your employees – it can be of high service to you as well. In the act of reading this discussion, you already grasp the larger picture of both the value and the procedure of the training. You can either participate daily in the general presentation of the program, or choose an accelerated learning and reinforcement system.

Toward this goal we offer several options:

ONE: A 2-day intensive executive seminar limited to 20 participants where you learn the full experience of the WizeWell Process in 4 three-hour seminar presentations led by a master teacher of the WizeWell Process.

TWO: You can schedule an executive training seminar or series of seminars in-house at your company, for high-power training of your senior management.

THREE: For individual executive training and reinforcement, you can be assigned a senior WizeWell coach to be at your service for as long as needed, in assuring that you and key members of your team fully master and implement the Process.

A Higher Vision At Work

The universal challenge that we must resolve in order to continue to thrive upon this planet is clear: we must all learn at work how to manage our own mental and emotional mind sets so that we can readily assume conscious responsibility for our thoughts, moods and actions on a moment to moment basis. That's what's required in order to be more healthy, innovative, compassionate and successful.

Furthermore, the new higher vision of work in America and throughout the world is that we're all working together to survive and prosper on this planet. We're all intrinsically caught up in this economic game together.

- Even though we play continual games of competition to keep us on our toes performing at our top level, all wise leaders know that cooperation is the name of the current game on this planet.

And this new vision of work indicates that that we need to learn how to expand our sense of business-as-usual so that we stop wasting valuable energy on conflict and stress, mental confusion and out-dated attitudes, and instead focus on more cooperative, mutually-supportive, high-health approaches to the at-work experience.

The WizeWell Process has been created by optimists. We see a bright light of reason and insight leading in positive directions if we trust and follow that light. And the light is human attention itself.

When we regularly aim that attention inward to our universal source of wisdom and right action, and then respond accordingly, we become beacons of light in our company and community.

As we're sure you know, that's what being a leader is all about – staying in touch daily or even hourly with your inner voice of reason and wisdom, and making sure that your employees do likewise.

~~~~~~~~~~~~~~~~~~

'Remember To Remember' Strategies

Beyond the formal 6-week training program, there are four available ways to maximize the ongoing impact of the WizeWell Process in your company's work life. Each day, we recommend that your employees fully utilize these 'remember to remember' strategies:

1: Audio/Video Mini-Reminders

For each of the 30 Focus Phrases, we've developed short (one-minute) mini-experiences that employees can now tap into anytime, anywhere, via audio, iPad, computer, smart phone, etc. For instance, they can go online (www.WizeWell.com) to the list of Focus Phrases, click on the one that draws their attention the most at that moment – and enjoy the guided experience.

- We also offer an online 'spin the wheel' Focus Roulette game where pure chance and serendipity choose a Focus Phrase for an employee to experience. They go to WizeWell.com and spin the wheel … and gain access to several different presentations of the Focus Phrase that appears for them at that moment.

2: The WizeWell Flash Cards

This set of 36 beautiful nature-photo Flash Cards, which employees can receive before or after completing the 6-Week WizeWell Process, will be an employee's best friend in remembering to bring Focus Phrases to mind. Hopefully they can make room on their desk for these Cards in their physical format, and reach for them at least once or twice a day, to effortlessly select a Focus Phrase to view, say to themselves, and hold in the back of their mind as they go about their work.

3: Musical Breath Reminders

When an employee finishes the formal 6-week WizeWell Process, they also receive full access to what are called MBRs (musical breath reminders). Because staying aware of one's breathing as much as possible throughout the workday is vital to overall well-being at work, we've developed this highly- effective musical support system for employees to include throughout each day at work.

- These quiet Musical Breath Reminders are short, enjoyable, and nonintrusive, and play on any of the various music delivery systems. Employees can program them to recur on whatever schedule they like, from every five minutes to once every hour. There are over 100 musical reminders, varying from 5 seconds to 20 seconds. They've been performed on soothing acoustic instruments, and employees can choose from a list of musical genres to match their taste and situation.

Whatever an employee is busy doing, when they hear one of these quiet Musical Breath Reminders, they just continue with their work ... but at the same time expand their awareness to include the experience of their breathing and whole-body presence. As they've learned in the WizeWell program, this expansion into present-moment mindfulness works wonders to relax their breathing, increase the oxygen and energy in their system, sharpen their mind, and brighten their mood.

4: The Wisdom-Wellness Spiral

After the first 6-week round of the WizeWell Process, your employees will find it highly beneficial to go another round on what we call the Wisdom-Wellness Spiral, revisiting each

Focus Phrase again – this time from a deeper, more expanded perspective. Also, employees who didn't participate the first time around, can enter at this second round.

- Each of the 30 WizeWell Focus Phrases offers an entire extended realm of ever-expanding experience, reflection, insight, and guidance. Many insights and experiences emerge only in the second or third or fourth round on the WizeWell Spiral.

~~~~~~~~~~~~~~~~~~

A combination of the four reminder-reinforcement choices just mentioned will serve your employees best as they advance through the next weeks and months. As they continue to take full advantage of our various online community and support programs, they will actively reap the long-term permanent benefits of the WizeWell Process.

The 4 Daily Breather Breaks

Throughout, the most important challenge is to make sure that employees continue to pause for the 4 Breather Breaks during each workday. Make sure this becomes a solid permanent routine, so that everyone on your team periodically shifts into that calm relaxed mental and emotional mindset that nurtures higher productivity and wellness. As they tap regularly into previously-buried reserves of energy, creativity, compassion, and enjoyment, everyone wins – Breather Breaks are your company's lifeline to a healthier, more successful and more enjoyable future.

~~~~~~~~~~~~~~~~~~

At-Home Programs

~~~~~~~~~~~~~~~~~

There are pragmatic limits to any at-work program, no matter how relevant the program might be to success at work. Therefore some of your employees might have found, while moving through their first engagement with the WizeWell Process, that a number of personal questions, emotions, and issues arose which weren't adequately explored.

- Your employees are complex emotional and spiritual beings, with many old unresolved emotional issues and a vast potential for inner growth and awakening – but at work they're being paid to hold their focus of attention primarily in directions that serve their company's everyday production goals.

At the same time, as we've seen, an emotionally healthy and happy employee represents the optimum team player. So for employees who want or need to explore the deeper aspects of emotional recovery and integration, plus learn to accelerate the evolution of their attitudes and habits toward more trust, compassion, insight, and realization, WizeWell offers a professional set of at-home and couples programs.

This at-home personal-support system will guide interested employees steadily and enjoyably toward attaining a brighter emotional and cognitive presence, so that they come to work with a higher clarity of mind and emotions. As with the entire WizeWell program, these at-home programs draw solidly from both cognitive science and the world's great meditative traditions, and are free of any philosophical or religious bias.

~~~~~~~~~~~~~~~~~

Online Conversations & Community

~~~~~~~~~~~~~~~~~~~

Many people find it extremely helpful, while exploring the WizeWell Process, to share their questions, struggles, insights and breakthroughs with a community of people who're also moving through the same process. To fulfill this need, we've created our long-term online community.

- Whether your company sets up an internal online team discussion, or employees join the larger WizeWell online community, there are numerous ongoing discussions of all six of the primary WizeWell themes, as well as an entry-point into the at-home programs.

Emotional growth and personal awakening require employees to focus during Breather Breaks temporarily away from the world around them, and look directly inward to their inner core of wisdom, guidance, and inspiration. However, the equal and opposite is also true in a well-balanced life: people need regular interaction with colleagues to order to reflect upon, understand, and integrate their Focus Phrase experiences more clearly.

A genuine sense of community naturally emerges when employees share their individual insights as they continue to discover new depths of compassion and realization – and this community is an essential part of the WizeWell vision.

There are a number of options for you to choose from, regarding how this community aspect of the WizeWell program is implemented in your company.

~~~~~~~~~~~~~~~~~~~

Scientific Verification Documents

~~~~~~~~~~~~~~~~~~~

The WizeWell Process represents a new-generation specialty advancement of Mindfulness-based Cognitive Therapy (MBCT), Mindfulness-based Stress Reduction (MBSR), Mindful Sport Performance Enhancement (MSPE) and Cognitive-based Stress Reduction (CBSR). During the last decade, a large number of research studies funded by NIH etc. have verified the scientific observations upon which the WizeWell Process is based. The following 57 medical and psychological research studies document seven key WizeWell principles:

> 1: The root cause of psychological stress at work results from a fixation on habitual worried thoughts about difficult business projects, job security, and other anxiety-laden situations. often provoked by chronic time pressure. Mindfulness-based re-focusing techniques can significantly reduce this causal factor of at-work stress.

> 2: Multitasking and undisciplined focal habits generate a great deal of lost productivity in the workplace. Proper mental training to strengthen positive focal patterns can be a major determinant in boosting productivity.

> 3: Chronic work stress increases the incidence of heart disease, diabetes, obesity, depression, and other diseases. Employee wellness and satisfaction can be directly improved through regular employment of the active psychological process identified in mental-silence methods and mindfulness meditation.

> 4: Insightful innovative thinking is negatively impacted by chronic stress at work. Innovative thinking can be nurtured at work through the proper inclusion of mindfulness-

based cognitive-focus programs.

5: Regular refocusing of attention toward positive thoughts and hopeful expectations, through the use of focus-phrase insertions, will generate related improvement in employee performance, wellness, empathy, and other key at-work variables.

6: Mindfulness-based training and meditation methods, when modified and employed for at-work implementation, will actively reduce employee anxiety, depression, fatigue, and stress.

7: The process of cognitive shifting from a mental to a perceptual focus will predictably stimulate a rapid shift in brain activity from past-future to present-moment experience, inducing a physiological reduction in anxiety and stress.

For full scientific verification of these statements, please read through the following research studies:

NASA/TM—2004–212824; Stress, Cognition, and Human Performance; Mark A. Staal Ames Research Center, Moffett Field, California; August 2004

The Effects of Time Pressure on Performance

This paper documents that in previous research, time pressure has been found to degrade performance across a variety of cognitive domains: judgment and decision making, visual search behavior, vigilance and attentional processes; memory recall strategies; concession making and integrative agreements; and subject's self-ratings of performance. In addition to a general drop in performance, time pressure and the corresponding sense of urgency experienced tends to result in strategy-shifting in teams;

task-shedding; tunneling of attention, and a speed/accuracy trade-off in performance.

~~~~~~~~~~~~~~~~~~

Mindfulness Meditation & Insightful Problem-solving

Sci China Life Sci. 2011 Oct;54(10):961-5. Epub 2011 Oct 29. Ren J, Huang Z, Luo J, Wei G, Ying X, Ding Z, Wu Y, Luo F.; College of Education, Zhejiang Normal University, Jinhua 321004, China. renj@zjnu.cn

Forty-eight university students were recruited to learn a simple meditation technique, and then given a list of 10 insight problems to solve. Results showed that relative to the control group, the groups who learned meditation solved significantly more problems, providing direct evidence for the role of meditation in promoting insight. Also, maintaining a mindful and alert state during meditation (raising a hand to report every 10 deep breaths compared to every 100 deep breaths) resulted in more insight regarding the items from the pre-test session. This implies that it was watchfulness in meditation, rather than relaxation, that contributed to insight.

~~~~~~~~~~~~~~~~~~

BMC Public Health. 2011 Apr 7;11:215.

Cost-effectiveness of internet-based cognitive training

Andersson E, Ljótsson B, Smit F, Paxling B, Hedman E, Lindefors N, Andersson G, Rück C.; Department of Clinical Neuroscience, Stockholm Center for Psychiatry Research, Karolinska Institutet, Stockholm, Sweden. erik.m.andersson@ki.se

Irritable Bowel Syndrome (IBS) is highly prevalent and is associated with a substantial economic burden. Mindfulness-based cognitive behavior therapy (CBT) has been shown to be effective in treating

IBS. The aim of this study was to evaluate the cost-effectiveness of a new treatment alternative: internet-delivered CBT based on exposure and mindfulness exercises. Significant cost reductions were found for the online treatment. Results were sustained at 3-month and 1 year follow-up. Internet-delivered CBT appears to generate health gains in IBS treatment and is associated with cost-savings.

~~~~~~~~~~~~~~~~~

Neuroimage. 2011 Aug 15;57(4):1308-16. Epub 2011 Jun 6.

Enhanced Brain Connectivity In Meditation Practitioners

Luders E, Clark K, Narr KL, Toga AW; Department of Neurology, UCLA School of Medicine, Los Angeles, CA 90095-7334, USA. eileen@loni.ucla.edu

Very little is currently known about the cerebral characteristics that underlie the complex processes of meditation. This new study used diffusion tensor imaging (DTI) data of high angular and spatial resolution plus atlas-based mapping methods to investigate white-matter fiber characteristics in a well-matched sample of long-term meditators and controls (n=54). Results showed pronounced structural connectivity in meditators compared to controls throughout the entire brain within major projection pathways, commissural pathways, and association pathways. The largest differences were within the corticospinal tract, the temporal component of the superior longitudinal fasciculus, and the uncinate fasciculus. These cross-sectional studies elucidate possible links between meditation and white matter fiber characteristics, indicating that long-term mental focusing in meditation somehow impacts the physical brain; future research is needed to explore this connectivity factor and its implications for both medical and psychological theory and applications.

~~~~~~~~~~~~~~~~~

J. Intl Soc. Life Info Sci. Vol. 28, No.1, March 2010

Mental Silence: Changing The Definition of Meditation

Ramesh MANOCHA, Deborah BLACK, David SPIRO, Jake RYAN and Con STOUGH; The University of Sydney, (Sydney, Australia) Institute of Psychiatry, King's College London (London, UK

This paper reports that until recently, the U.S. National Center for Complementary and Alternative Medicine (NCCAM) defined meditation as "a conscious mental process that induces a set of integrated physiological changes termed the relaxation response". Recently the NCCAM has reviewed its understanding of meditation by including a new central feature: "In meditation, a person learns to focus his attention and suspend the stream of thoughts that normally occupy the mind." This definition indicates a shift from a physiological ("relaxation-response") to an experiential (suspension of thinking activity) definition, more in line with traditional eastern understandings.

A recent research project by the authors of the paper explored the physiological implications of this paradigmatic shift. A mental-silence orientated form of meditation (Sahaja yoga, SYM) was compared to rest. Throughout the meditation period mean ST of the SYM group decreased while that of the Rest group increased. After ten minutes of meditation, 13 of the 16 meditators manifested a reduction in ST compared to baseline whereas 7 of the 10 participants in the control group manifested an increase compared to baseline. The study suggests that the experience of mental silence and rest are not psychophysiologically identical despite the fact that they are overtly similar. Implications of this, and need for further evaluation, are discussed, along with the need for more specific and effective experimental techniques for inducing the state of mental silence in a research environment.

~~~~~~~~~~~~~~~~~~

Am. Diabetes Association; August 2009

Stress at Work Doubles the Risk of Type 2 Diabetes

Alexandros Heraclides, MSC, Tarani Chandola, PHD, Daniel R. Witte, PHD and Eric J. Brunner, PHD; From the Department of Epidemiology and Public Health, Royal Free and University College London Medical School, London, U.K.

The intent of this study was to investigate the effect of psychosocial stress at work on risk of type 2 diabetes, adjusting for conventional risk factors, among a sample of British, white-collar, middle-aged men and women. Emerging as a prospective analysis (1991–2004) from the Whitehall II cohort study, this research studied a sample of 5,895 Caucasian middle-aged civil servants free from diabetes at baseline. Type 2 diabetes was ascertained by an oral glucose tolerance test supplemented by self-reports at baseline and four consecutive waves of data collection including two screening phases. Standard job strain and iso-strain models were used to assess psychosocial work stress. The research data concluded that psychosocial work stress was a primary independent predictor of type 2 diabetes among women after a 15-year follow-up.

~~~~~~~~~~~~~~~~~

Int. J. of Psychological Therapy; Volume 11 Num. 2 - June 2011- P 285-296

Mindfulness-based Cognitive Therapy (MBCT) Reduces Depression and Anxiety Induced by Stressful Setting

Hossein Kaviani , Foroozan Javaheri

A randomized, controlled study was conducted in a non-clinical population to investigate the impact of mindfulness-based cognitive therapy (MBCT) on depression, anxiety, automatic thoughts, and dysfunctional attitudes, normally induced by exam as a real stressful setting. The results indicated that MBCT was effective at helping participants to deal with their anxiety and depressive feelings before, during and after stressful circumstances. In addition, the reductions in negative automatic thoughts and dysfunctional attitudes in those who received MBCT were significant. The findings provide further evidence that MBCT might be a useful intervention for enhancing well-being in non-clinical populations who are susceptible to experience anxiety and depression in real life situations.

~~~~~~~~~~~~~~~~~~

Drug Alcohol Depend. 2011 Dec 1;119(1-2):72-80. Epub 2011 Jul 1.

Mindfulness Training For Smoking Cessation

Brewer JA, Mallik S, Babuscio TA, Nich C, Johnson HE, Deleone CM, Minnix-Cotton CA, Byrne SA, Rounsaville BJ.; Department of Psychiatry, Yale University School of Medicine, New Haven, CT 06510, USA.

Cigarette smoking is the leading cause of preventable death in the world. Mindfulness training (MT) has begun to show benefits in a number of psychiatric disorders, including depression, anxiety and more recently, in addictions. However, until his research, MT had not been evaluated for smoking cessation. In this study, 88 treatment-seeking nicotine-dependent adults were randomly assigned to either receive MT, or the Am. Lung Association's freedom from smoking (FFS) treatment. Compared to those randomized to the FFS intervention, individuals who received MT showed a greater rate of reduction in cigarette use during treatment and maintained these gains during follow-up. They also exhibited a trend toward greater point prevalence abstinence rate at the end of treatment (36% vs. 15%, p=.063), which was significant at the 17-week follow-up (31% vs. 6%, p=.012). This study indicates that mindfulness training may confer benefits notably greater than those associated with current standard treatments for smoking cessation.

~~~~~~~~~~~~~~~~~~

Reducing Job Stress May Prevent Depression

By Nancy Schimelpfening, About.com Guide   April 29, 2009

The link between at-work stress and recurrent depression has already been established in various medical studies. And according to a study in the May 1, 2009 issue of the *American Journal of Epidemiology*, reducing one's job stress may lower the risk of depression. The study found that, over a period of ten years, employees who initially reported that their jobs were stressful, but later reported feeling that their jobs had become less stressful, were at the same risk of developing depression as those workers who had felt their jobs were low-stress the entire time. The researchers point out that, in any given 30-day period, 4.4% of U.S. workers have major depression. These results indicate that interventions targeted to reducing job stress may significantly reduce the risk of depression. The investigators also found that, of those who reported consistently high job stress during the study, 8% had an episode of major depression at some point during the study, compared to 4% of those who had low job stress during the entire time period.

~~~~~~~~~~~~~~~~~~

Positive-Psychology Research Overview

Based on review articles and research of Martin Seligman and Tracy Steen, Psychologhy Department, University of Pennsylvania; June, 2010;

Some years ago, the American Psychologist magazine focused its millennial issue on the emerging science of positive psychology, referring to the study of positive emotion, positive character, and positive institutions (Seligman & Csikszentmihalyi, 2000). Advancing beyond pioneering work by Rogers (1951), Maslow (1954, 1962), Jahoda (1958), Erikson (1963, 1982), Vaillant

(1977), Deci and Ryan (1985), and Ryff and Singer (1996) and others, recent research has shown that individuals who maintain a positive psychological outlook on life are more successful in their work and their private lives, and enjoy a higher level of wellness, than people who focus overmuch on the negatives of life. (e.g., Cameron, Dutton, & Quinn, 2003; Easterbrook, 2003; Gardner, Csikszentmihalyi, & Damon, 2001; Kahneman, Diener, & Schwarz, 1999; Murray, 2003; Vaillant, 2000).

~~~~~~~~~~~~~~~~~

Organizational Dynamics, Vol 33(4), 2004, 338-351.

The Role of Psychological Wellbeing in Job Performance

Wright, Thomas A.; Cropanzano, Russell

As the authors of this paper discuss, for decades since the Hawthorne studies, the happy/productive worker thesis has been under active discussion by management scholars and business executives. According to this key premise of management research, workers who are happy on the job will have higher job performance than those who are less happy. Happiness at work has been measured in terms of job satisfaction. This paper explores research considering worker happiness as psychological well-being (PWB). The studies show that an increase in happiness, considered as PWB, works to the benefit of both employers and the employees. They offer intervention strategies for promoting workplace happiness and increased productivity.

~~~~~~~~~~~~~~~~~

Med Educ. 2011 Apr;45(4):381-8

The Effects of Mindfulness Practice on Stress Levels

Warnecke E, Quinn S, Ogden K, Towle N, Nelson MR.; Menzies Research Institute, University of Tasmania, Hobart, Tasmania, Australia.

This study's goal was to determine whether the practice of mindfulness reduces the level of stress experienced by senior medical students. Results showed that mindfulness practice reduced stress and anxiety in senior medical students. Stress is prevalent in medical students and can have adverse effects on both student health and patients. The authors conclude that a simple, self-administered, evidence-based intervention now exists to manage stress in this at-risk population.

Statistical Report On Employee Satisfaction

By Susan. Heathfield, Human Resources; About.com Guide; March 2010

Reports show that Americans of all ages and income brackets continue to grow increasingly unsatisfied with their work situation, as evidenced in report by *The Conference Board*. The report, based on a survey of 5,000 U.S. households conducted by *TNS*, finds only 45% of those surveyed say that they are satisfied with their jobs, down from 61.1% in 1987, the first year in which the survey was conducted. The percentage of employees satisfied with their jobs is lowest in the under 25 age group with only 35.7% satisfied. In the age group 25-34, 47.2% are satisfied; age 35-44 scored 43.4% in job satisfaction; in the 45-54 age range scored 46.8%; employees 55-64 scored 45.6% and age 65 and over, 43.4% are satisfied. The downward trend in job satisfaction raises issues about the overall engagement of America's workforce, and employee productivity, retention, creativity, risk-taking, and overall employee motivation and interest in work.

~~~~~~~~~~~~~~~~~~

Mindfulness Practice Increases Brain Gray-matter Density

Psychiatry Res. 2011 Jan 30; 191(1):36-43. Hölzel BK, Carmody J, Vangel M, Congleton C, Yerramsetti SM, Gard T, Lazar SW. Source: Massachusetts General Hospital, Harvard Medical School, Boston, MA.

Mindfulness-Based Stress Reduction (MBSR), a widely-employed mindfulness training program, has been reported to produce positive effects on psychological well-being and to ameliorate symptoms of mental and physiological disorders. A controlled longitudinal study has now investigated pre-post changes in brain gray matter concentration attributable to participation in an MBSR program. Anatomical magnetic resonance (MR) images from 16 healthy, meditation-naïve participants were obtained before and after they underwent the 8-week program. MR analyses confirmed increases in gray matter concentration within the left hippocampus, plus increases in the posterior cingulate cortex, the temporo-parietal junction, and the cerebellum in the MBSR group compared with the controls. The results suggest that participation in MBSR is associated with changes in gray matter concentration in brain regions involved in learning/memory processes, emotion regulation, self-referential processing, and perspective taking.

~~~~~~~~~~~~~~~~~~

Does happiness affect productivity?

Daniel Sgroi / July 26, 2010; VOX research-based policy analysis

One of the biggest growth areas in economics over the last few years has been "happiness economics". A plethora of intriguing results suggests that there is a link between mood and economic variables such as income or economic growth. Recent research indicates that a rise in happiness might change behavior at the micro-level, looking specifically at productivity. If happiness raises productivity by increasing workers' effort, then economists need to take the emotional state of economic agents more seriously, with more effective bridges built between applied psychology and applied economics. If happiness boosts human productivity, based on these productivity findings, we can expect happier people to very different economic agents from their less contented peers. *Easterlin, Richard (1974), Oswald, Andrew (1997; 2009), Proto, Eugenio, Daniel Sgroi, and Andrew Oswald (2010), Alex Dobson (2010)/*

~~~~~~~~~~~~~~~~~~

Evidence-Based Complementary and Alternative Medicine; Volume 2011 (2011), Article ID 960583, 8 pages:10.1155/2011/960583

Mental-Silence Meditation Reduces Work Stress, Anxiety and Depression in Full-Time Workers

R. Manocha, D. Black, J. Sarris, and C. Stough; Department of Psychiatry, Sydney Medical School, Australia;

The intent of this study was to assess the effect of mental-silence meditation on work stress, anxiety and mood in full-time workers. 178 adult workers participated in an 8-week controlled trial comparing a "mental silence" approach to meditation to a "relaxation" active control and a wait-list control. Results indicate a significant improvement for the meditation group compared to both the relaxation control and the wait-list groups. This suggests that mental silence-orientated meditation is a safe and effective strategy for dealing with work stress and depressive feelings. The findings suggest that "thought reduction" or "mental silence" may have specific effects relevant to work stress and hence occupational health.

~~~~~~~~~~~~~~~~~~

Short-Term Meditation: At Work Benefits

October issue of the Proceedings of the National Academy of Sciences (2007; 104 [43], 17152–56).

One of the limitations for employing effective meditation practice, especially in the workplace, has been a perceived lack of time needed to include meditation in a busy routine. A study conducted in China has shown that meditating as little as 20 minutes daily over a 10-day period can improve both focus of attention, and quality of mood. Integrative body-mind training (IBMT) combines a number of traditional techniques including body relaxation, breath adjustment, mental imagery, and mindfulness training accompanied by background music. Chinese researchers developed IBMT as a way to simplify meditation and mindfulness training, making it easier for adults and children alike. Both before and after the training, subjects took tests to measure their levels of stress, anxiety, depression and anger. Stress hormone levels were also measured. Subjects in the IBMT short-form meditation group exhibited more stable moods, less stress and anxiety, and lower levels of stress hormones than those in the relaxation group.

~~~~~~~~~~~~~~~~~

National Center For Complementary & Alternadtive Medicine, NIH

Mental-Silence Effects – Research Overview

The Meditation Research Program of NIH's National Center for Complementary and Alternative Medicine (NCCAM) has recently funded a number of research projects focused on scientific evaluation of the so-called 'mental silence phenomenon' that is predictably elicited by mindfulness meditation. The practice of mindfulness essentially involves the passive observation of internal and external stimuli without mental reaction. In mental-silence meditation, meditators also progress to a state of no mental content at all. Findings so far at NCCAM suggest that mental silence attained through meditation is associated with a specific detectable effect. For example, a rigorous study of meditation used to reduce occupational stress showed significantly superior effects on measures of work-related stress and depressive feelings, when compared to an active control. In this and other studies, mental silence appears to generate an improvement in psychological parameters and quality of life, greater than with conventional stress management. These studies suggest that the mental silence experience may be associated with a specific pattern of central and peripheral physiological activities associated with specific effects that are clinically beneficial.

~~~~~~~~~~~~~~~~~

BBC NEWS, July 7, 2007

Stressful Job Linked to Depression and Anxiety

This British study showed that having a high-pressure job doubles the risk of depression and anxiety in young adults. A study of 1,000 32-year-olds found 45% of new cases of depression and anxiety were attributable to stressful work. They defined a highly demanding job as involving a lack of control, long hours, non-negotiable deadlines, and a high volume of work. The report in *Psychological Medicine* concluded that employers need to do more to protect workers' mental health. Overall 10% of men and 14% of women in the study suffered a first episode of depression or anxiety over the year-long study. But the risk was double in those with the highest pressure jobs. Research leader Dr Maria Melchior, epidemiologist at the Institute of Psychiatry, Kings College London, stated that: "Our study shows that work stress appears to bring on diagnosable forms of depression and anxiety in previously healthy young workers."

~~~~~~~~~~~~~~~~~

Neuroimage. 2011 Aug 15;57(4):1524-33.

Neural Responses In Mindfulness Meditators

Taylor VA, Grant J, Daneault V, Scavone G, Courtemanche J, Lavarenne AS, Beauregard M.; Centre de Recherche en Neuropsychologie et Cognition (CERNEC), Département de Psychologie, Université de Montréal, Montréal, Québec, Canada.

As presented in this paper, there is now solid evidence that mindfulness meditation is beneficial for the treatment of mood and anxiety disorders, but so far, little is known about the neural mechanisms through which mindfulness modulates emotional responses. This important brand-new functional magnetic resonance imaging study investigates the effects of mindfulness on the neural responses to emotionally laden stimuli, and examines the impact of mindfulness training on the brain mechanisms supporting the processing of emotional stimuli. The findings indicate that for experienced meditators, mindfulness induced a deactivation of default-mode network areas across all valence categories, and did not influence responses in brain regions involved in emotional reactivity during emotional processing. For beginners relative to experienced meditators, mindfulness induced a down-regulation of the amygdala during emotional processing. These findings indicate that the long-term practice of mindfulness leads to emotional stability by promoting acceptance of emotional states and enhanced present-moment awareness, rather than by eliciting control over low-level affective cerebral systems from higher-order cortical brain regions. These results have implications for affect-related psychological disorders,, and for emotional wellness in general.

~~~~~~~~~~~~~~~~~~

Meditation and Pain Relief

From the April 6, 2011 edition of the Journal of Neuroscience: Fadel Zeiden PhD; Wake Forrest Baptist Medical Center;

This ASL-MRI brain-scan study of mindfulness meditation related to physical pain demonstrated a 40% reduction in pain intensity and a 57% reduction in pain unpleasantness. In the study, mindfulness meditation produced a greater reduction in pain than even morphine or other pain-relieving drugs, which typically reduce pain ratings by about 25%. Meditation also increased brain activity in areas including the anterior cingulate cortex, anterior insula and the orbito-frontal cortex, the areas that shape how the brain builds an experience of pain. The more that these areas were activated by meditation, the more that pain was reduced. The authors suggest that is so effective in blocking pain because it reduces pain at multiple levels of processing. Zeidan and colleagues believe that meditation has great potential for clinical use because so little mindfulness-meditation training was required to produce such dramatic pain-relieving effects.

~~~~~~~~~~~~~~~~~

Journal of Clinical Sport Psychology, 2011, 5, 99-116

Mindful Sport Performance Enhancement (MSPE)

Rachel W. Thompson, Keith A. Kaufman, Lilian A. De Petrillo, Carol R. Glass, and Diane B. Arnkoff The Catholic University of America

The purpose of this research was to evaluate the long-term effects of mindful sport performance enhancement (MSPE), a program designed to improve athletic performance and psychological aspects of sport. One-year follow-up assessments were conducted on archers, golfers, and long-distance runners who attended 4 mindfulness workshops. Across the athlete groups, participants reported significant increases in the ability to act with awareness (an aspect of trait mindfulness) and overall trait mindfulness from pretest to follow-up, along with significant decreases in task-related worries and task-irrelevant thoughts (both aspects of cognitive interference during sport). The long-distance runners exhibited significant improvement in their mile times from pretest to follow-up, with significant correlations between change in runners' performance and trait variables. Results suggest that MSPE is a promising intervention associated with long-term changes in trait variables that may contribute to optimal athletic performance.

~~~~~~~~~~~~~~~~~

The *Journal of Occupational and Environmental Medicine*, *January 2010*.

Study Connects Workplace Stress and Obesity

Medical studies indicate that approximately 32 percent of adult men and 35 percent of adult women are obese in this country. When the prevalence of overweight and obesity are combined, 68 percent of adults fit the category (72 percent prevalence among men; 64 percent among women), according to a recent report in the *Journal of the American Medical Association*. Stressful working conditions are known to impact health behaviors directly and indirectly. Directly, stress can affect the neuroendocrine system, resulting in abdominal fat, for example, or it may cause a decrease in sex hormones, which often leads to weight gain. Indirectly stress is linked to the consumptions of too many fatty or sugary foods and inactivity.

A new study by the University of Rochester Medical Center observed that chronic job stress and lack of physical activity are strongly associated with being overweight or obese. Lead researcher Diana Fernandez, M.D. at the URMC Department of Community and Preventive Medicine said her study is among many that associate high job pressure with cardiovascular disease, metabolic syndrome, depression, exhaustion, anxiety and weight gain.

Mindful Attention Prevents Impulsive Behavior

Esther K. Papies, Department of Psychology, Utrecht University, Netherlands; Lawrence W. Barsalou, Detp. of Psychology, Emory University, Atlanta, GA, USA

In three related studies, the researchers demonstrated that mindful attention can reduce impulsive action. Participants received a brief mindfulness procedure in which they observed their reactions to external stimuli as transient mental events, rather than subjectively real experiences. Participants then applied this procedure to highly attractive food items. Reactions to food stimuli were assessed. Across experiments, spontaneous reactions elicited by attractive food were eliminated in the mindful-attention condition compared to the control condition. These findings suggest that mindful attention to one's own mental experiences helps to control impulsive responses; these findings suggest that mindfulness is a potentially powerful method for facilitating self-regulation related to appetite and weight loss etc.

~~~~~~~~~~~~~~~~~~

Research Review: Meditation Effects On Perception

Studies at NIH/NCCAM (http://nccam.nih.gov/) have shown that meditation has both short-term and long-term positive effects on various perceptual faculties. In 1984, Brown *et al.* conducted a study that measured the absolute threshold of perception for light stimulus duration in practitioners and non-practitioners of mindfulness meditation. The results showed that meditators have a significantly lower detection threshold for light stimuli of short duration. In 2000, Tloczynski *et al.* studied the perception of visual illusions (Poggendorff Illusion) by zen masters, novice meditators, and non-meditators. The zen masters experienced a statistically significant reduction in initial illusion (measured as error in millimeters) and a lower decrement in illusion for subsequent trials. These results indicate that a person who meditates comes to perceive objects more as directly-experienced stimuli, and less as concepts. Through this reduction of cognitive stimuli and increase in perceptual awareness, meditation can therefore influence both the quality (accuracy) and quantity (detection) of perception." Of note: in 2006 NCCAM revised their definition of meditation, emphasizing the experience of the "suspension of thought activity" as primary. It has been found that all approaches to meditation can achieve non-specific benefits; however, the mental silence approach may be associated with additional specific positive alterations which are clinically beneficial.

~~~~~~~~~~~~~~~~~~

Society For Human Resource Management; Nov 15. 2009; Kathy Gurchiek

Research Links Workplace Practices and Employee Health

New studies presented at an Oct. 13, 2009, congressional briefing in Washington, D.C. demonstrate that interactive advancements in the workplace environment can benefit employee health and company profit. In 2005, studies at NIH showed how training supervisors to be more supportive of employees' family and personal lives led to higher job satisfaction and better physical health, plus reduced the likelihood of turnover. In a related study of 658 employees at Best Buy, those who were granted increased control over work schedules and decision-making showed a 45 percent reduction in turnover; job satisfaction increased and unnecessary work was reduced.

~~~~~~~~~~~~~~~~~~

J Experimental Psychol Gen. 2011 Sep 12.

Mindfulness Training Positively Affects Attention

Jensen CG, Vangkilde S, Frokjaer V, Hasselbalch SG.

In a blinded design, 48 meditation novices were randomly assigned to either a mindfulness-based stress reduction (MBSR), a non-mindfulness stress reduction (NMSR), or an inactive control group. Selective attention in the MBSR group improved significantly more than in any other group. Similarly, only the MBSR intervention improved the threshold for conscious perception and memory capacity. Furthermore, the MBSR group showed significantly less physiological stress, while increasing their mindfulness levels significantly. This demonstrates that mindfulness-based stress reduction techniques may contribute uniquely to attentional improvements.

~~~~~~~~~~~~~~~~~

J. of Child 7 Family Studies; February 2011

The Effectiveness of Mindfulness Training for ADHD

Saskia van der Oord, Susan M. Bögels and Dorreke Peijnenburg

This study evaluated the effectiveness of an 8-week mindfulness training for children aged 8–12 with ADHD, and parallel mindful parenting training for their parents. Parents ($N = 22$) completed questionnaires on their child's ADHD and ODD symptoms, their own ADHD symptoms, parenting stress, parental overreactivity, permissiveness and mindful awareness before, immediately after the 8-week training and at 8-week follow-up. Training was delivered in group format. There was a significant reduction of parent-rated ADHD behavior of themselves and their child from pre-to posttest and from pre- to follow-up test. Further, there was a significant increase of mindful awareness from pre-to posttest, and a significant reduction of parental stress and overreactivity.

The study shows preliminary evidence for the effectiveness of mindfulness for children with ADHD and their parents.

~~~~~~~~~~~~~~~~~~~

Personality and Individual Differences; Volume 51, Issue 2, July 2011, Pages 166-171

Nature Connectedness: Associations With Wellbeing And Mindfulness

Andrew J. Howell[,] , Raelyne L. Dopko, Holli-Anne Passmore, Karen Buro; Grant MacEwan University, Edmonton, Alberta, Canada.

Wilson's (1984) biophilia hypothesis predicts that people's psychological health is associated with their relationship to nature. Two current studies examined associations among nature connectedness, well-being, and mindfulness in samples of undergraduate students. Significant associations emerged among measures of nature connectedness and indices of well-being (in Study 1 and Study 2) and mindfulness (in Study 2). Results indicate that there is a definite impact of the experience of nature connectedness upon healthy individuals, and also that this variable of nature connectedness might prove to be a valuable tool in encouraging mental and physical health health.

~~~~~~~~~~~~~~~~~~~

Corporate Leadership Council / Corporate Executive Board: July 2003

Research Summary On Employee/Customer Satisfaction

Research quantifying the links between employee satisfaction and customer satisfaction, productivity, and financial performance began in 1980 with Benjamin Schneider's survey of satisfaction levels of bank customers and employees. Studies such as Frederick Reichheld's "The Loyalty Effect," (1996) and James Heskett, W. Early Sasser, and Leonard Schlesinger's "The Service Profit

Chain" (1997) and ongoing research have demonstrated direct quantifiable links between customer service variables (satisfaction and loyalty), employee variables (satisfaction, enthusiasm, commitment, capability), and financial results. These and related studies indicate that: unhappy employees are less productive and more likely to have higher absence rates; satisfied employees are more productive, innovative, and loyal; increases in job satisfaction lead to increases in employee morale, which lead to increased employee productivity; employee satisfaction leads to customer retention. Over 40% of the companies listed in the top 100 of *Fortune* magazine's "America's Best Companies to Work For" also appear on the *Fortune 500*.

~~~~~~~~~~~~~~~~~~

SALARY.COM: Employee Turnover/Satisfaction Stats

According to a Salary.com poll, in 2006/2007 employers estimated replacement costs due to turnover to average approximately $15,000 per employee. This year employers estimate costs will average $21,000 which represents a 40% increase.

The following list from the poll shows the five main reasons employees name for staying in a job:

> Relationships with co-workers: 31%
> Relationship with manager(s): 22%
> Desirable working hours: 17%
> Attractive compensation: 23%
> Attractive benefits: 18%

This poll indicates the prime importance of purposefully focusing on relationship solidarity at work, in order to keep valued employees in a company.

~~~~~~~~~~~~~~~~~~

Br. J. of Clinical Psych, Sept 2011

Mindfulness And Acceptance-based Interventions for Anxiety Disorders

Jon Vøllestad, Mort Birke Nielsen, Geir Høstmark Nielsen

Mindfulness and acceptance-based interventions (MABIs) are receiving increasing attention in the treatment of mental disorders. These interventions might be beneficial for patients with anxiety disorders, but no prior reviews have comprehensively investigated the effects of these type of intervention on clinical samples. The aim of this study was to review and synthesize extant research on MABIs for patients with diagnoses of anxiety disorders. The researchers conducted a systematic search of relevant databases according to pre-defined criteria. Studies were eligible for inclusion if they employed MABIs for patients diagnosed with anxiety disorders. The conclusion of the review of research papers was as follows: MABIs are associated with robust and substantial reductions in symptoms of anxiety and depressive symptoms. More research is needed to determine the efficacy of MABIs relative to current treatments of choice, and to clarify the contribution of various processes of mindfulness and acceptance to observed outcome.

~~~~~~~~~~~~~~~~~~

ScienceDaily (Jan. 23, 2006)

Work Stress Leads To Heart Disease And Diabetes

Studies show that stress at work is an important risk factor for the development of heart disease and diabetes. In a recent study published by the British Medical Journal, stress at work was clearly linked with heart disease. Researchers examined the association between work stress and the metabolic syndrome (a cluster of factors that increases the risk of heart disease and type 2 diabetes) in 10,308 British civil servants aged between 35 and 55, over a 14 year period. A clear relation was found between exposure to job stress and the metabolic syndrome, even after adjusting for other risk factors. Prolonged exposure to work stress may affect the nervous system, and chronic stress may reduce biological resilience and thus disturb the body's physiological balance (homoeostasis). This study provides evidence for the biological plausibility of psychosocial stress mechanisms linking stressors from everyday life with heart disease.

~~~~~~~~~~~~~~~~~

J Consult Clin Psychol. 2011 Oct;79(5):618-28.

Mindfulness Training Increases Momentary Positive Emotions In Adults Vulnerable To Depression

Geschwind N, Peeters F, Drukker M, Graduate School for Neuroscience, Department of Psychiatry and Psychology, Maastricht University Medical Centre, 6200 MD Maastricht, the Netherlands.

This study aimed to examine whether mindfulness-based cognitive therapy (MBCT) increases momentary positive emotions, and the ability to make use of natural rewards in daily life. The results were positive throughout. From this and other studies, MBCT is clearly associated with increased experience of momentary positive emotions, as well as greater appreciation of, and enhanced responsiveness to, pleasant daily-life activities. These changes were unlikely to be pure epiphenomena of decreased depression and, given the role of positive emotions in resilience against depression, may contribute to the noted protective effects of MBCT against depressive relapse.

~~~~~~~~~~~~~~~~~

European Heart Journal, August 1, 2007

Work Stress and Coronary Heart Disease

Tarani Chandola[1,*], Annie Britton[1], Eric Brunner[1], Harry Hemingway[1], Marek Malik[2], Meena Kumari[1], Ellena Badrick[1], Mika Kivimaki[1] and Michael Marmot[1] [1]Department of Epidemiology and Public Health, University College London, [2]Department of Cardiac and Vascular Sciences, St George's University of London, London, UK

The purpose of this medical research was to determine the biological and behavioral factors linking work stress with coronary heart disease (CHD). A total of 10 308 London-based male and female civil servants aged 35–55 at phase 1 (1985–88) of the Whitehall II study were studied. Exposures included work stress (assessed at phases 1 and 2), and outcomes included behavioral risk factors (phase 3), the metabolic syndrome (phase 3), heart rate variability, morning rise in cortisol (phase 7), and incident CHD (phases 2–7) on the basis of CHD death, non-fatal myocardial infarction, or definite angina. The statistical analysis indicated that chronic work stress was associated with CHD, and this association was stronger among participants aged under 50. Work stress can be seen as an important determinant of CHD among working-age populations, mediated through indirect effects on health behaviors and direct effects on neuroendocrine stress pathways.

~~~~~~~~~~~~~~~~~~

J. NZ Med Ass, 08 July 2011, Vol 124 No 1338
Jillian Simpson, Tim Mapel

Health Benefits of Mindfulness-based Stress Reduction (MBSR) for Chronic Physical Illness

This study's aim was to establish the value of Mindfulness-based Stress Reduction (MBSR) for people with chronic health problems in managing symptoms and coping with their illness. Twenty-nine participants completed a wait-list control study. Physical and psychological health and well-being were measured before, after, and 6 months after the 8-week training program using a variety of internationally recognized screening tools. The study showed statistically-significant improvements in almost all categories measured. MBSR clearly offers health benefits for chronic illness sufferers. Used as an economical and effective adjunctive therapy for decreasing morbidity associated with chronic illness, MBSR provides both clinicians and patients with an additional option for the better management of chronic illness.

~~~~~~~~~~~~~~~~~

Scope of Stress in the American Workplace

NIOSH Publication No. 99-101; Steven Sauter; Larry Murphy; Michael Colligan; Naomi Swanson; Joseph Hurrell; Frederick Scharf, Jr.

This report explores how the very nature of work is changing at overly-rapid speed, and how now more than ever before, job stress poses a threat to the health of workers. Job stress has become a common and costly problem in the American workplace, leaving few workers untouched. In a recent study, 25% of employees view their jobs as the number one stressor in their lives (*Northwestern National Life*); 75% of employees believe the worker has more on-the-job stress than a generation ago (*Princeton Survey Research Associates*); and problems at work are more strongly associated with health complaints than any other life stressor –more so than even financial problems or family problems (*St. Paul Fire and Marine Insurance Co.*).

~~~~~~~~~~~~~~~~~

Mindfulness Journal; Volume 2, Number 4, 236-241

Effects of Mindfulness Training on Driving Performance

Steven J. Kass, Lisa A. VanWormer, William L. Mikulas, Shauna Legan and David Bumgarner

In this study, mindfulness training was examined in relation to drivers' situation awareness and performance. University students enrolled in a Buddhist psychology class were taught concentration techniques in which they were instructed to focus their attention on their breath, and mindfulness techniques in which they learned to objectively notice whatever arises in consciousness. These students were to practice these techniques in their everyday activities in order to improve their mindfulness and concentration. Compared with a control group, these students scored significantly higher on a scale used to assess their ability to concentrate, and their situation awareness in a driving simulator. These results indicate that mindfulness training might significantly impact actual driving performance over time, by improving drivers' awareness of their environment, and enabling them to block out distractions and quickly identify hazards.

~~~~~~~~~~~~~~~~~

Aliment Pharmacol Ther. 2011 Aug; 34(3):363-73.

Mindfulness Training For Gastrointestinal Anxiety Relief

Kearney DJ, McDermott K, Martinez M, Simpson TL. VA Puget Sound Health Care System, Seattle, WA 98108, USA. David.kearney@va.gov

Stress perception and GI-specific anxiety play key roles in irritable bowel syndrome (IBS). Mindfulness-based stress reduction (MBSR) is a widely available stress-reduction course. The aim of this study was to determine whether participation in MBSR would be associated with improvement in bowel symptoms, GI-specific anxiety, and IBS-Quality of Life. In the study, participation in

MBSR was associated with improving IBS-related quality of life and GI-specific anxiety. In related research, a randomized controlled trial explored the feasibility and efficacy of a group program of mindfulness training for women with (IBS). The technique involves training in intentionally attending to present-moment experience and non-judgmental awareness of body sensations and emotions. This parallel trial also demonstrated that mindfulness training has a substantial therapeutic effect on bowel symptom severity, improves health-related quality of life, and reduces distress. The beneficial effects persist for at least 3 months after group training.

Social Work Education; Volume 30, Issue 6, 2011

Mindfulness, Health and Wellbeing

Maria Napoli & Robin Bonifast, pages 635-649

In this paper, the authors explain how social-work students experience stress, emotional exhaustion and vicarious trauma during their education, and how these reactions can negatively impact their ability to objectively integrate course material. Studies have shown that when social work students are mindful in the classroom (present without internal or external filters) they're better able to regulate emotions, and are more open to diverse perspectives. As such, mindful practice can help enhance practice skills, especially those related to tuning in to clients. This paper describes the elements of a mindful classroom, introduces a framework for teaching mindful practice, and presents the results of a research study that examined learning outcomes associated with this framework. Graduate students participated in a 16-week course that focused on enhancing self-care and professional development via the use of mindful practice strategies. Four skill areas were tested: acting with awareness, observing, accepting without judgment, and describing. Results indicate that students significantly increased their use of mindfulness in the first three.

~~~~~~~~~~~~~~~~~

Journal of Religion & Spirituality in Social Work: Volume 30, Issue 3, 2011 pg 212-233; ; *Tessa McGarrigle & Christine A. Walsh PhD*

Mindfulness, Self-Care, and Wellness in Social Work

The demands placed on human service workers in supporting people through challenging circumstances can contribute to high levels of stress and burnout. Self-care practices implemented regularly may decrease the impact of the high levels of stress while also serving as strategies for coping during particularly stressful times. The interconnections between contemplative practices, including mindfulness, as coping and preventative strategies for self-care practice among human service workers are beginning to emerge. This research examined the effectiveness of 8 weeks of contemplative-practice training in increasing self-care, awareness, and coping strategies. Scores on the Perceived Stress Scale and the Mindfulness Attention/Awareness Scale showed that mindfulness was significantly increased, and stress significantly decreased, over the intervention.

~~~~~~~~~~~~~~~~~~

European Society of Cardiology; UCL Epidemiology & Public Health 23 Jan 2008

Stress At Work Linked To Heart Disease

This research presents strong evidence of how work stress is linked to the biological mechanisms involved in the onset of heart disease. Published in the *European Heart Journal,* the research is the first large-scale study to look at the cardiovascular mechanisms of work stress; it provides the strongest evidence yet of the way stress at work can lead to coronary heart disease (CHD). Dr Tarani Chandola, a senior lecturer in UCL Epidemiology & Public Health and the lead author of the study, concluded that stress at work is definitely related to an increased risk of coronary heart disease. The study found that stress can lead to CHD either directly by activating stress pathways between the nervous system, the endocrine glands and their hormones, or indirectly via its association with unhealthy lifestyles.

~~~~~~~~~~~~~~~~~~

Behav Cogn Psychother. 2011 May;39(3):349-53.

Mindfulness Groups In Psychosis Treatment

Jacobsen P, Morris E, Johns L, Hodkinson K.; South London and Maudsley NHS Foundation Trust, UK.

Although early psychiatric pioneers such as Humphrey Osmond at the New Jersey Neuropsychiatric Institute performed meditation experiments with schizophrenic patients with partial success, mindfulness meditation is just now being re-introduced clinically for people with distressing psychosis. Pragmatically, is this type of treatment successful? The present study aimed to investigate the feasibility of running and evaluating a mindfulness group on an inpatient ward for individuals with chronic and treatment resistant psychosis. Eight participants attended a 6-week mindfulness group on a specialist tertiary inpatient ward. This study demonstrated that mindfulness exercises were acceptable, and were also well-tolerated by participants. This research is just a bare beginning of exploration in applying meditative techniques for the treatment of mental illness.

~~~~~~~~~~~~~~~~~~

Cognitive and Behavioral Practice; April 2011

Mindfulness in the Treatment of Suicidal Individuals

Jason B. Luoma, Jennifer L. Villatte, Portland Psychotherapy Clinic, Research, and Training Center, Portland, OR.

This paper reviews the fact that suicidal behavior is exhibited by a diverse population of individuals, and spans many diagnostic categories. A growing body of data suggests that experiential avoidance, or the tendency to escape or avoid unwanted psychological experiences, even when such efforts cause harm, may represent a universal process the leads to suicidal behavior. This article discusses theory and evidence that support mindfulness and psychological acceptance as a means to target experiential avoidance in suicidal clients, and thereby reduce the risk of suicide. The article also provides case examples of the application of mindfulness to suicidality, and discusses how mindfulness may help clinicians in managing the stress associated with treating suicidal clients.

~~~~~~~~~~~~~~~~~~

Brain Res Bull. 2011 May 30;85(3-4):96-103. Epub 2011 Apr 8.

Effects of Mindfulness Training on Anticipatory Alpha Modulation in Primary Somatosensory Cortex

Kerr CE, Jones SR, Wan Q, Pritchett DL, Wasserman RH, Wexler A, Villanueva JJ, Harvard Osher Research Center, Harvard Medical School, Boston, MA 02215, USA. cathy.catherinekerr@gmail.com

As the authors of this paper explain, during selective attention, alpha rhythms are modulated in early sensory cortices, suggesting a mechanistic role for these dynamics in perception. They then investigate whether alpha modulation can be enhanced by mindfulness meditation (MM), a program training practitioners in sustained attention to body and breath-related sensations. Using magnetoencephalographic (MEG) recording representation, meditators demonstrated enhanced alpha power modulation in response to a cue. This finding is the first to show enhanced local alpha modulation following sustained attentional training, and implicates this form of enhanced dynamic neural regulation in the behavioral effects of meditative practice.

~~~~~~~~~~~~~~~~~

Respir Physiol. 1989 Feb;75(2):199-209.

Individuality of Breathing Patterns Assessed Over Time

Benchetrit G, Shea SA, Dinh TP, Bodocco S, Baconnier P, Guz A.,
Laboratoire de Physiologie, Faculté de Médecine de Grenoble, France.

In this early breath/personality research, subjects underwent two studies separated by 4-5 years to test whether their resting pattern of breathing was reproducible over time. A statistical analysis concluded that the individuality of breathing pattern is maintained over a long period. The conclusion is that how we breathe is to a certain extent who we are – and to change our breathing patterns is to change our personality, at certain levels.

~~~~~~~~~~~~~~~~~

Respir Physiol. 2000 Sep;122(2-3):123-9.

Breathing Pattern In Humans: Individuality

Benchetrit G. Laboratoire de Physiologie Respiratoire Expérimentale, Théorique et Appliquée; Faculté de Médecine de Grenoble, Université Joseph Fourier, 38700, La Tronche, France. gila.benchetrit@imag.fr

In this follow-up study of adult awake human subjects at rest, it was found that there exists a diversity in the breathing pattern not only in terms of tidal volume and inspiratory and expiratory duration and derived variables, but also in the airflow profile. Each individual appears to select one particular pattern among the infinite number of possible combination of ventilatory variables and airflow profile. This one particular pattern appears to be a relatively stable characteristic of an adult individual being reproducible in several conditions, and after a long period of time.

~~~~~~~~~~~~~~~~~~

Gen. Hosp. Psychiatry (1995) 17:192-200.

Mindfulness-Based Stress Reduction for Anxiety

Miller, J., Fletcher, K. and Kabat-Zinn, J. Three-year follow-up and clinical implications of a mindfulness-based stress reduction intervention in the treatment of anxiety disorders.

As this paper discusses, a previous study by the authors of the paper, of 22 medical patients with DSM-III-R-defined anxiety disorders, demonstrated both clinically and statistically significant improvements in subjective and objective symptoms of anxiety and panic following an 8-week outpatient physician-referred group stress reduction intervention based on mindfulness meditation. A 3-year follow-up comparison of this cohort with a larger group of subjects from the intervention who had met criteria for screening for the original study suggests generalizability of the results obtained with the smaller, more intensively studied cohort. Ongoing compliance with the meditation practice was also demonstrated in the majority of subjects at 3 years. The authors herein conclude that an intensive but time-limited group stress-reduction intervention based on mindfulness meditation can have long-term beneficial effects in the treatment of people diagnosed with anxiety disorders.

~~~~~~~~~~~~~~~~~~

Int J Psychophysiol. 1997 Sep;27(2):153-9.

Anxiety And Respiratory Patterns: Their Relationship

Masaoka Y, Homma I. Second Department of Physiology, School of Medicine, Showa University, Tokyo, Japan.

This study investigated the effect of mental stress on respiration, using unpleasant sounds. The purpose of this study was to investigate ventilatory response in emotions caused by mental stress and physical load, and to determine the relationship between respiratory pattern and personality. Results indicate that respiratory patterns respond to mental stress in predictable patterns related to tense shallow breath cycles. These findings offer important evidence relating respiratory-function response to psychological aspects of stress.

~~~~~~~~~~~~~~~~~

Psychooncology. 2010 Sep;19(9):1004-9.

Psychological Benefits for Cancer Patients in Mindfulness-based Stress Reduction (MBSR)

Birnie K, Garland SN, Carlson LE. Department of Psychosocial Resources, Tom Baker Cancer Centre, Calgary, AB, Canada.

As described in this research paper, cancer patients experience many negative psychological symptoms including stress, anxiety, and depression. This distress is not limited to the patient - their partners can also experience many psychological challenges. Mindfulness-based stress reduction (MBSR) programs have demonstrated clinical benefit for a variety of chronic illnesses, including cancer. This is the first study to report MBSR participation with partners of cancer patients. Overall, the MBSR program proved itself of value for improving psychological functioning and mindfulness, for both members of the couple. Future research is suggested to further explore potential benefits of joint couple attendance in the MBSR program.

~~~~~~~~~~~~~~~~~

J Am Acad Nurse Pract. 2008 Apr;20(4):212-6.

Mindfulness-based Stress Reduction: Clinician's Guide

Praissman S. Johns Hopkins Bayview Medical Center, Baltimore, Maryland.

This report surveys the recent research on mindfulness interventions. The aim here is to provide nurse practitioners (NPs) with clinical research about Mindfulness-Based Stress Reduction (MBSR) and demonstrate its usefulness for reducing stress in a variety of populations. The survey concludes that, based on the scientific evidence, MBSR is an effective treatment for reducing the stress and anxiety that accompanies both daily life, and chronic illness. Research in nursing situations has also shown that MBSR is helpful for healthcare providers, reducing work-related stress and enhancing their interactions with patients. No negative side effects from MBSR have been documented.

~~~~~~~~~~~~~~~~~

J Altern Complement Med. 2008 Apr;14(3):251-8.

Comparing Mindfulness-based versus Cognitive-behavioral Stress Reduction Techniques

Smith BW, Shelley BM, Dalen J, Wiggins K, Tooley E, Bernard J. Department of Psychology, University of New Mexico, Albuquerque, NM.

The objective of this pilot study was to compare the effects of two mind-body interventions: the recently-developed mindfulness-based stress reduction (MBSR) and the more traditional cognitive-behavioral stress reduction (CBSR). The former differs primary from the latter by the inclusion of mindful-meditation dimensions of the treatment, focusing on present-moment mental silence as a primary active element of the treatment. MBSR was an 8-week course using meditation, gentle yoga, and body scanning exercises to increase mindfulness. CBSR was an 8-week course using cognitive and behavioral techniques to change thinking and reduce distress. MBSR subjects improved on all eight outcomes, CBSR subjects improved on six of eight outcomes. Multivariate analyses showed that the MBSR subjects had better outcomes across all variables.

~~~~~~~~~~~~~~~~~~~

Overview of the 30 Core Focus Phrases:

~~~~~~~~~~~~~~~~~

Focus Phrases are realistic statements of universal human intent, pointing one's attention and creative power toward inner experiences that stimulate wellness, wake up latent talent and potential, and align one's personal life with universal human values and aspirations. Regularly holding a Focus Phrase in mind will predictably generate progress toward personal well-being and, at the same time, company success.

There are six primary categories of employee wellbeing that we address here; therefore the program covers six weeks of training and guidance. Within each of these six themes are four primary psychological highlights to focus daily attention upon, plus a summary statement at the end of each week to take home for the weekend.

In the same way that a plant requires water and sunlight in order to flower, Focus Phrases require ongoing present-moment awareness of one's breathing and whole-body presence in order to become active.

- The first week of the WizeWell Process teaches a stress-reduction method for staying aware of one's breathing experience while saying a Focus Phrase. Hold in mind that Focus Phrases are said silently to yourself on the exhale and then, on the inhale, you focus on the experience elicited by the words of the Focus Phrase. You can devote 1 to 4 breaths for each Focus Phrase.

Every moment in life is new and unique – so every time you say a Focus Phrase to yourself, you will naturally have a new experience. You'll find that each Focus Phrase builds on the previous ones so that, over time, the Focus Phrases gain a steadily-increasing power to elicit deeper and more significant experience and growth:

"Physical Wellbeing" ... *reducing stress – boosting inner presence*

"I choose to enjoy this moment."
"I feel the air flowing in and out of my nose."
"I feel the movements in my chest and belly as I breathe."
"I'm aware of my whole body, here in this present moment."
"I choose to breathe, relax, and feel good."
~~~~~~~~~~~~~~~~~~~

"Emotional Wellbeing" ... *regaining inner balance and harmony*

"I feel the emotions in my face ... throat... heart... and belly."
"I let go of all the stress and worry, and feel peaceful inside."
"I accept the world just as it is, right now."
"I honor and love myself ... just as I am."
"I choose to accept and integrate all of my feelings. "
~~~~~~~~~~~~~~~~~~

"Creative Wellbeing" ... *stimulating innovation and higher purpose*

"I am open to receive ... guidance and insight."
"I feel connected with my creative Source."
"I am here to serve, to love, to prosper, and enjoy myself."
"I am ready to act with courage and integrity."
"I choose to focus on inspiration, purpose, and wisdom."
~~~~~~~~~~~~~~~~~~

"Productive Wellbeing" ... *augmenting manifestation power*

"My mind is quiet ... I feel calm and connected."
"I am in touch with my deeper needs."
"My creative vision is perfect and complete."
"Each new moment is manifesting my vision."
"I choose to create what's really needed."
~~~~~~~~~~~~~~~~~~

"Interactive Wellbeing" ... *nurturing trust and mutual acceptance*

"I am a good listener."
"I accept everyone I work with ... just as they are."
"I trust my spontaneous thoughts and expressions."
"I feel safe, confident, and valued on my team."
"I choose to participate in trust, joy, and harmony."
~~~~~~~~~~~~~~~~~~

"Integrated Wellbeing" ... *maximizing health and fulfillment*

"I feel in touch with my authentic presence."
"I welcome the creative playfulness of my inner child."
"I work fast and efficiently – but I don't hurry."
"I have deep reserves of energy and compassion."
"I choose to feel calm, bright, healthy, and whole. "
~~~~~~~~~~~~~~~~~~

About the Authors

John Selby is a psychologist, cognitive inventor. executiv counselor, author, and awareness-management pionee He has written over two dozen business-success an psychology books published in 14 languages with over hal a million books in print. Early in his career he conducte mind-management and mindfulness-meditation researc for NIH and the New Jersey Neuro-Psychiatric Institut developing innovative approaches to stress relief, insomni treatment, cognitive shifting and short-form mindfulnes meditation. He was educated at Princeton University, UC Berkeley, The Graduat Theological Union, and the Radix Institute.

Among John's numerous psychological innovations are his Focus Phrase stress reduction technologies, at-work cognitive shifting techniques, and 'Quiet Minc innovation methods. Drawing on over a hundred cognitive-research studies, John book titles include Executive Genius, Take Charge Of Your Mind, Listening Wit Empathy; Secrets Of A Good Night's Sleep, Quiet Your Mind, and his new boo with Greg Voisen, Wisdom, Wellness, and Redefining Work. John is the creator th WizeWell Process and co-owner of WizeWell Systems. He lives and works in Sant Cruz, California.

Greg Voisen is an author, speaker and founder of Inside Personal Growth a podcast program reaching thousands on topics including personal growth, wellness, mastery and spirituality. Greg has interviewed over 400 thought leaders in these fields and has broadcast over 300 hours of recorded podcasts in the last five years. He holds a BA degree in Business Management from San Diego State University, and a Master Degree in Spiritual Psychology from the University of Santa Monica.

With a personal passion for fitness and wellness in the business arena, Greg worke for 20+ years designing and implementing medical plans for small to medium-siz businesses, and observed the system of healthcare delivery becoming more an more dysfunctional. Integrating his in-depth understanding of personal growth psychology, and business pragmatics, Greg joined forces with John Selby to co author Wisdom, Wellness and Redefining Work in order to raise awareness of th root cause of stress in the workplace, and generate positive change in coping wit stress to reduce medical costs and improve overall employee performance.

WizeWell
UNLEASHING VITALITY

www.ingramcontent.com/pod-product-compliance
Lightning Source LLC
Chambersburg PA
CBHW060458280326
41933CB00014B/2786